A Mother's Courage

MALKA LEVINE

MACMILLAN

First published 2023 by Macmillan
an imprint of Pan Macmillan
The Smithson, 6 Briset Street, London EC1M 5NR
EU representative: Macmillan Publishers Ireland Ltd, 1st Floor,
The Liffey Trust Centre, 117–126 Sheriff Street Upper,
Dublin 1, D01 YC43
Associated companies throughout the world
www.panmacmillan.com

ISBN 978-1-0350-2500-8 HB
ISBN 978-1-0350-2501-5 TPB

1 3 5 7 9 8 6 4 2

A CIP catalogue record for this book is available from the British Library.

Page 8 bottom © Stephen Miles, ARPS. All others images courtesy of the author.

Typeset in Sabon by Jouve (UK), Milton Keynes
Printed and bound by CPI Group (UK) Ltd, Croydon, CR0 4YY

Visit **www.panmacmillan.com** to read more about all our books
and to buy them. You will also find features, author interviews and
news of any author events, and you can sign up for e-newsletters
so that you're always first to hear about our new releases.

For David, Elaine, Avi, Marianne, Max and Louis

Contents

Prologue

November 1942

I was cold, hungry and scared. Around me in the prison yard the guards were yelling, shoving people to form a line, hitting them with the butts of their guns or prodding them with sharp metal spikes fixed to heavy poles. Men, women and children were pushed onto trucks and driven away. Some were mute, others sobbing. Children were screaming and hiding under the skirts of their mothers, babies were crying for food.

Standing with my mother, Grandma Miriam and two older brothers, I could not take in the magnitude of the catastrophe. I was three and a half years old and what most concerned me was the biting cold that seized my body and numbed my fingers, stopping me from buttoning my coat. I tugged on my mother's skirt, demanding her attention. 'Mum, mum, help me!'

My mother was only too aware that our fate was sealed. We were just minutes away from being forced onto a truck that would take us to our deaths. Fourteen months earlier, 15,000

Jews from our home town of Ludmir had been taken away by truck, perhaps the very same ones we saw today. They were driven to land near a village called Piatydni and mowed down, their bodies left in a mass grave. For over a year my mother had fought to shield her three children in the ghetto. She had faced down the corrupt head of the Jewish council to demand a work permit that offered some protection, had crawled out at night under the barbed wire fence that surrounded the ghetto to scavenge food from the fields for us to eat, had kept us hidden from the SS and Gestapo who had no use for children and no hesitation in eliminating them.

Each day that gave us a tiny chance to live was another short victory that fuelled her determination to save us. And yet, when I begged her to do up my buttons in the prison yard, she didn't respond. For the first time, she was swept by a sense of futility. What does it matter, she thought, if my child catches cold? We were on the last leg of our lives' journey and all her reserves were gone.

April 2023

While I am the storyteller, I am not the story. This book is not about me but about those people who saved me. And while it is set in a very small city in western Ukraine, the message is a universal one – that even in the darkest of days, the human spirit can triumph over despair and courage will conquer fear.

My mother was burdened by three young children in the midst of genocide. Her chances of survival were practically nil.

In Ludmir there were about 25,000 Jews when the German army arrived and only about thirty alive when they left, of which nine were children. My two brothers and I made up three of the nine. We survived due to my mother's resourcefulness, courage and determination, but also because others put themselves at risk so we would live. Some were people we had never met before such as a German Wehrmacht officer who freed us from the prison yard that day. Others were acquaintances. The most remarkable, an old Ukrainian couple called the Yakimchuks, gave us shelter on their farm. Alas, so many years have passed that all my heroes have long gone but I am humbled now to put their deeds onto the page and preserve them for generations to come.

No one knows exactly how many Jews were killed in present-day Ukraine but it has been estimated that 1.5 million died, about a quarter of the six million who lost their lives in the Holocaust and the highest percentage of any country. Some historians believe the total is higher. We were considered subhuman by the Nazis and not worth counting, so this uncertainty will always remain. In any case, this is not a contest over numbers. Each life was precious. The majority of Jews in Ukraine were not transported to concentration camps but instead the Nazis rounded up thousands of people at a time and shot them. It was highly organized mass murder, accomplished with German precision. The calamity was that some of the indigenous population, like the Poles and the Ukrainians themselves, took part in the massacre – just as a few of them saved Jewish lives. The brave people who helped us thought for themselves rather than listening to anti-Semitic venom, and let compassion be their guide.

It is the responsibility of democratic institutions to quench the fire before it gets out of control. As I write this prologue, in the heart of Europe, Russia is raging a senseless war against Ukraine. Both are Slavic countries, with the same traditions, the same Orthodox religion. There is nothing that divides them, apart from the sick ambitions of one of their leaders, Russia's President Putin. It is inconceivable that even today there are autocrats who go to war for no good reason, just for self-glorification. In news reports from Ukraine we see civilians being targeted and killed by Russia with chilling indifference. War crimes are being committed by Russian soldiers with the aim of terrifying the population into compliance. We see hatred of Ukrainians, and the West, being whipped up by President Putin's propagandists in the Russian media. There are many examples of ethnic and religious hatred leading to violence around the world. We must reach out to the people at the receiving end so that evil never triumphs.

My mother often talked about our past, sometimes with a sardonic twist that made me chuckle. Her stories are central to this book. I had a fair amount of input from my big brother Haim who has more detailed memories of the early war years than I do. He is so inspirational, a kind soul who is generous with his time. My middle brother, Shalom, is very inward; he finds it hard to talk about our experiences in the Holocaust but he is very good on the wider picture of the Second World War. I have to be a bit careful not to bring up dark memories but he is only too willing to help.

I have also used historical information from a remarkable book my mother gave me years ago, *Ludmir's Diary*, as well as the more recent *Jewish Ludmir*, by Volodymyr Muzychenko, which has many first-hand accounts from those who witnessed the atrocities. Reading these testimonies made me both shudder and rage again at the inhumanity displayed.

Today I am eighty-three years old and live in a tranquil suburb of Nottingham. I feel privileged to be in England. I love the country and I love the people, especially their sense of humour. I even like the English weather – never too hot, never too cold, always just right. But I still have flashbacks to Ludmir to a time when men lost their sanity and killing Jews was legal.

Chapter 1

Hinterland

When I was born, my father held me in his arms and danced around the room, happy to have a daughter at last. My brother, Shalom, who was five at the time, told me this as I was writing this book and it comforts me to know that I brought my father joy. I like to think of my family as they were then, living their ordinary lives in Ludmir, untouched by war. I can picture my Dad puffing on his pipe in his bicycle shop on Farnah Street, in a huddle of eager men debating the top speed of the latest model from Italy. And I can just see my mother, a basket over one arm, walking briskly along Kovelska Street, with its tiny Jewish shops in a neat row, their rooves arched, their wares crammed into the window. Her eye would invariably be caught by a trader, perhaps selling the brightly coloured china that appealed to her naive country-girl taste. When Ludmir was covered in snow, my brothers would attach ropes to my little sledge and pull me along the quiet streets, as I shrieked with glee and my cheeks burned red in the icy air.

It is over seventy-five years since I left the quintessentially

Jewish city of Ludmir but it still has a hold on my imagination. It too was a victim of the Nazis. The city's official name was Volodymyr-Volynskyi (named after Prince Vladimir the Great who founded it in the late tenth century), and it is situated in what today is north-western Ukraine. The arrival of skilled Jewish merchants in the twelfth century, with trading in their DNA, saw Ludmir flourish after years of poverty. They came seeking safety when crusaders in Western Europe turned against the Jews. The Jewish magnate Benjamin Hendis arrived in the twelfth century, Isaac of Ludmir came two centuries later, and I often wonder if Shakespeare's Shylock was based on those well-known merchants. Strong ties were established with Western Europe and Byzantium, and the city became the cultural and economic centre of Kievan Rus'.

Occupying a strategic gateway between the West and the riches of the East meant that the city grew and flourished but her location also meant that she was wide open to external aggression. In the thirteenth century, the Mongols brutally invaded, setting the pattern for attacks by other nations over subsequent centuries. Situated close to the borders of the two great powers of Poland and Russia, Ludmir lived on the edge, geographically and metaphorically, and it changed hands many times. The Poles and Ukrainians were constantly at each other's throats, and the city was destroyed several times by despots, tyrants and decadent monarchies; and yet, miraculously, again and again, Ludmir bounced back, re-emerging even stronger and more robust than before.

Even as wars raged, Ludmir stayed open for business. Merchants took locally produced goods to the Eastern markets to sell, bringing back precious silk, spices, camphor oil – used in medicine and as an insect repellent – and, the most lucrative of all, arms. As the town grew, craftsmen arrived from neighbouring cities and Ludmir's marketplace buzzed with merchants speaking Turkish, Italian, Russian and Ukrainian but, most of all, Ludmirian Yiddish. It had a special ring of money. In 1569, the city passed from Lithuanian to Polish rule, and by the eighteenth century, the Jews of Ludmir were dealing mainly in horses which they imported from Hungary and sold to the Poles for their cavalry – a niche profitable market. As the local tailors were also renowned, they jumped on the opportunity to sell clothing to the Polish soldiers.

Ludmir was annexed to the Russian empire in 1795 after Poland lost its independence. Life under tsarist Russia was harsh, with heavy taxes levied on the population, but the Jews as usual muddled through. Their life was mainly governed by the many learned and revered rabbis of Ludmir, who had perhaps too much sway given that their judgement was sometimes tragic. Ludmir possessed many men of mind and too few of might.

In the opening years of the twentieth century, when my parents were born, many charities were set up to help the old and the dispossessed. A hospital and pharmacy were established, and a special bank created to give loans to new enterprises. The new library was named after Sholem Alaichem, a renowned Yiddish author whose most famous book, *Tuvia the Milkman and His Seven Daughters*, was the inspiration for *Fiddler on the Roof*. Performing artists started to come to the city which became more sophisticated and avant-garde. The arrival of the railway in 1906 was a game-changer, giving Ludmir access to the cities of Poland and Russia, and as adults my parents frequently made the 100-kilometre journey to the busy markets and shops of the Hapsburg city of Lemberg (known today as Lviv). This large, sophisticated metropolis made Ludmir look like an over-grown village.

As children my parents also experienced the turmoil of the First World War. Ludmir was occupied by Austrian forces in 1915, during which time the population suffered from a shortage of food and poor sanitary conditions that led to illness. Many Jews were taken away as forced labour, and there were big demonstrations in protest. When news reached the Austrian parliament, the order was given to return the men. Alas, on the way back home some were murdered. The governor of Ludmir, an Austrian officer called Mozer, ensured that those responsible were hanged in the centre of the city.

The Russian Revolution of 1917 led to the toppling of the tsar and, in the political vacuum that followed, mayhem ensued. In Ludmir a militia of 400-strong was established to protect the grain warehouses. The group had 200 Jewish representatives, and 100 each of ethnic Poles and Ukrainians. The Jewish majority should have ensured peace between the other parties, but the Poles were busy grabbing land on behalf of the newly independent Polish state and the Ukrainians wanted independence – and both wanted to take Ludmir, which had strategic importance thanks to the railway. When Ukrainian peasants and soldiers attacked Ludmir, the Jewish militia retaliated for once and the attackers were beaten and fled.

In January 1919, Polish platoons took the city and soon

committed their own atrocities, shooting people in the streets and cutting Jewish men's beards off, just like the Nazis who came after them. But being under Polish rule had some advantages for Ludmir's Jewish community, which was hooked up with the Jewry of Poland and grew in influence. Jewish political parties started to emerge in the city, a new Jewish school for 500 pupils was set up called Tarbut, followed by a large agricultural college of the same name. The city had a vibrant commercial centre based predominantly on agriculture, and grain in particular, and was also home to many skilled Jewish craftsmen.

My father, Moshe Fischmann, grew up in Ludmir and was a true townie. His father, who ran a bakery, died at quite a young age, leaving Grandma Miriam to bring up her five sons on her own. My mother, Rivka Akin, had a more affluent upbringing in the village of Lytovezh, about thirty kilometres south of Ludmir, where she lived on her father's large farm. As well as selling his own wheat, Grandpa Akin traded in grain, speculatively buying crops from local smallholders. He was prosperous enough to own a townhouse in Ludmir. The farm is no longer – it was torn down by ransackers, many of whom believed Jews stashed away precious items in the walls. The beautiful village of Lytovezh does remain, though, as do some of the trees that once graced the orchards of my grandfather's expansive estate.

My parents met at some point in the 1920s, their relationship not a *shidduch* (arranged marriage); there wasn't a matchmaker like *Fiddler on the Roof*'s Yente, which used to be very common back then. Mum and Dad fell in love, and it was true love; my mother went through hell with her father over it.

Grandpa Akin was a Chassid, so observed strict orthodox Judaism. He had eight children, two boys and six daughters, who were all taught at home by yeshiva – orthodox Jewish college – students from Vilnius, the crème de la crème. The girls were only expected to learn how to read and write, but my mother clearly listened to her brothers' lessons and had a detailed knowledge of the Bible and Hebrew theology and philosophy.

Obviously, the farmhouse was more like a matchmaking hub, and my grandparents would have been pleased if one of their daughters had fallen for these well-regarded scholars. My grandpa was a jolly man and famously generous with his hospitality, so his home was the place to be on Friday nights and on high holidays. Not only were his girls renowned for their beauty (my mother's violet-coloured eyes were certainly striking), but the yeshiva boys liked Grandma Hannah's kosher fare. They all failed to catch the attention of my mother, who instead fell for my father, which displeased Grandpa Akin, who wasn't too keen for his daughter to find her own *shidduch*. The main problem was that Dad was an *apikoros*, a non-believer, who saw Judaism and religion in general as just an amalgamation of superstitious tales. He was a liberal, forward-thinking man – dangerously modern in Grandpa's eyes! When Grandpa Akin found out that Mum wanted to marry Dad, he threatened not to provide a *nadn* (a dowry) for the union. 'Well, I would rather have the man,' my mother countered, displaying a strength of character unusual amongst her female peers. When his entreaties and arguments didn't work, Grandpa eventually relented, after many sleepless nights, and my parents married in around 1929, when my mother was twenty-one and my father in his mid-twenties. Three years later they welcomed my older brother Haim into the world, and another son, Shalom, in 1934. I was born in June 1939.

Despite Grandpa's initial objection to the marriage, he and my mother continued to be close. As she was the oldest of his children, she had started helping him on the farm at an early age, harnessing his horses and filling the sacks with wheat ready for the miller. She was a born merchant like her dad, and it was only natural that she would form a partnership with Grandpa Akin, buying fields of wheat and barley from local farmers. The wheat was used for bread and barley for brewing, the latter particularly popular during the long, harsh winters in our part of the world – what a convenient excuse! Mum encouraged Grandpa to concentrate more on barley, for which they received a better price.

My mother also worked closely with my father. They were not the traditional Jewish shtetl couple where the man goes off to work and the wife stays at home to look after the many children and make chopped liver and bless the candles on the sabbath. They were partners, both in marriage and at work, and together they built a life for themselves and their children. We lived in Dad's family home on Horodelska Street, where Grandma Miriam had her own separate quarters. I'm sure she had a lot to put up with when a new bride came into the family home. She wasn't used to dealing with girls, having five adoring sons around her.

At times the Akin clan would descend on the house, arriving in their horse-drawn wagon in summer and sleigh in winter when Grandma Hannah would be wrapped in a fine fur coat (something Grandma Miriam could not afford). Suddenly all would be hustle and bustle, as chaotic as a coaching inn, as the gifts were unloaded, usually fruit from the farm – apples, cherries or pears. According to Mum, Grandpa had the knack of making himself immediately at home (and the centre of attention). A good-looking, tall man, he had a lot of self-assurance. He would take out his Russian silver snuff box, ceremoniously place a pinch of snuff on his hand, take a deep sniff, then pull out a flask full of schnapps from his back pocket to have a reviving swig, before asking Grandma Hannah what she'd brought for lunch. Before we would sit down to eat, he'd wash his hands in the kitchen, come back to stand at the head of the table and bless the bread that we had been lucky to receive. I bet Dad was laughing inwardly and thinking, what a charade! Grandma Miriam felt pushed aside when the Lytovezh mob descended on the house.

My brothers and I spent a lot of time with Grandma Miriam, and she often looked after us when my parents were working. A practical, loving woman, she was quite progressive, considering her environment, and, like my father, was not particularly religious, which must have taken some getting used to for my mother, who had been brought up in a Chassidic home. I believe at times this was a source of some friction between Mum and Grandma, especially when it came to the pots and pans, which – according to Jewish laws – had to be strictly separated: some used for meat and some for dairy. This was second nature for Mum but Grandma couldn't give a hoot.

My dad's brother, Uncle Hirsch, also had an apartment in the building, so clearly there was plenty of room for the extended family. Mum and Dad took great pleasure in furnishing the house, though Mum was still a country girl at heart with a taste to match. On a trip to Lemberg, she fell for a pair of beds with heavy, ornate nickel frames. I can just imagine Dad saying 'very nice' as he often did (even if he didn't mean it) while his teeth gripped the stem of his pipe as he tried not to express his real feelings. Because he admired her, he gave in. There was also an opulent green velvet sofa that we children were not allowed to sit on. It was just for adults on Yom Tov (religious holidays). My defiant brothers would jump on mum's cherished sofa with their muddy shoes when she was out and I couldn't wait to snitch on them when she was back. This usually earned me a sharp – and well-deserved – slap from Haim and Shalom. I still owe them an apology.

Mum delighted in Oriental kilim rugs, some of which adorned the walls alongside the paintings Dad often bought on his travels. Shalom vividly remembers a painting brought back from Russia, depicting Napoleon sitting on a white horse outside the gates of Moscow. Of course, Napoleon, like Hitler, failed to conquer the Russian Empire, and similarly saw his reputation of invincibility shattered in the process. I suspect our house looked like the gilded contents of a Hapsburg junk shop.

My father was a businessman: he owned the city's biggest bicycle shop as well as an engineering works. Mum would stand in for him at the shop when he needed to be elsewhere. She was a dab hand at mending punctures, and she wasn't afraid of charging a good price for her services, unlike my dad, who was perhaps thinking about keeping his customers happy so they'd come back. In her work with Grandpa, Mum dealt in a much-needed commodity and didn't have to worry about competition.

Dad was also an egalitarian with an affinity for the less well-off, which is why he installed an oven at the back of our house where locals too poor to buy bread could come and bake their own. He made sure there was always plenty of dry chopped wood to stoke the flames. On Friday evenings, with the oven still hot and just right for slow cooking, they would flock with large black pots of cholent – stews of meat, potatoes and beans – which would simmer slowly throughout the night ready for the Shabbat feast. It was convenient for observant members of the congregation who were not permitted to light a fire on the sabbath – it was even a sin to switch on the electrics. Many of Dad's business ventures were a product of his passions: he loved to race bikes and enjoyed various outdoor sports, including rowing. He set up a kayak-hiring business on the River Luha – which flowed around the western side of the city – that his youngest brother, Uncle Joel, ran. Haim remembers skating on the river when it froze over during Ludmir's bitter winter months. When the weather started to warm and the ice to thin, he sometimes returned home minus a skate or even a shoe. I bet Mum was furious, but also relieved he hadn't fallen in the river. Both brothers had bicycles, a rarity in 1930s Ludmir, but one of the perks of having a father who sold them.

One of Dad's biggest achievements was the establishment of a matzo bakery, the city's first fully automated unit run entirely by electricity. It was in fact Mum's idea. One day, when she was busy counting her sacks of wheat, she turned to Dad and said,

'I have the grain, you have the brain. It would make good sense to have a factory for matzos. This will add additional value to my yields.' Dad creased up laughing, but the following morning told Mum enthusiastically: 'I'm up for it.' Poor Dad, he was probably relieved that she only wanted a bakery and not a brewery for her barley.

Dad took on the building of the factory and it was definitely no mean feat. Grandpa Akin did not believe it was doable. It needed a large amount of money that he certainly wasn't going to be ploughing into it. The remark of his that went down in family history was: 'Which sane Jew is going to buy chametz matzos kosher for Passover from an *apikoros* Bolshevik?' As Dad wasn't relying on Grandpa's financial benevolence, he took this on the chin.

It must have been a monumental task to build the whole structure himself from scratch. First the money, then the labour and sourcing all the equipment, which he would not have found locally. He drew up all the structural plans, including the electrics. And he wasn't too proud to mix the cement and build the brick walls himself. To save money, he got a few mates to come and help. There were furnaces, conveyor belts, lifts for the sacks of flours, and carousels going round and round with matzos. Any that cracked were made into matzo meal.

The factory did well, employing a few locals, non-Jewish and Jewish. In March, a month before Passover, the matzo factory would be working to full capacity, ready for the festive rush. As well as their customers in Ludmir, the produce would be distributed by rail to surrounding towns. Some was given to charity – an old people's home and an orphanage that my parents supported.

When the factory was ready to open, Grandpa Akin wouldn't come in as the entrance was not graced by a mezuzah (a case containing Hebrew verses that is traditionally placed in the doorways of Jewish homes).

'I was right not to lend you money for your fancy endeavour,' Grandpa said. 'What Jew will enter here to buy matzos if there's no mezuzah to bless?'

Dad must have been fuming as he never asked or expected Grandpa to chip in but he tried to make a joke of it for the sake of domestic harmony.

'What kind of mezuzah does the *mechuten* [father-in-law] want? Gold, silver, base metal, or one studded with gemstones?'

Grandad looked at his son-in-law, spread his arms wide with pride, and said, 'Thank God we live in Ludmir, where you can have any mezuzah you wish for. If you try to buy a rosary [knots or beads used in Catholic prayer], now that would be a challenge. You would have to go as far as Kiev.'

I think Grandpa Akin was a little envious of Dad, who was not shackled by his faith. The traditions that many like my grandfather so openly observed created that sense of a different and closed community that did not help the frequently strained relationship between us and the Gentiles we lived amongst. We felt that following kosher rituals and living according to the words of the Bible would ensure that God was in our midst, but as the Second World War loomed, it soon became abundantly clear that He was not. Our host country, Poland, was anti-Semitic to its core – its people already inured to brutality, their hostility to Jews in no way discouraged by the Holy See, which offered up a poisoned Catholic dogma that blamed Judaism for the world's ills. These prejudices, backed by papal pronouncements, created conditions ideal for a pogrom or two.

By 1939, Ludmir had about 40,000 inhabitants, 25,000 of whom were Jewish; the next most numerous group was the Poles, with the remaining minority largely Ukrainians. The proportion of Ukrainians in the surrounding villages was higher. Relations between the different sectors were sometimes amicable, albeit transactional – a Ukrainian might have his wheat ground in a Jewish-owned mill, buy his shoes from a Jewish cobbler and use the services of a Jewish doctor or dentist – but prejudice against Jews was deeply rooted and antagonism was dished out on a daily basis, by Poles and also Ukrainians to some degree.

Various members of my family, seeing no real future for themselves in Ludmir, emigrated in the 1930s, including two of my dad's brothers who headed to Palestine. Around fifty people from the city did the same, as part of the Zionist movement that had already sprung up in Ludmir, which encouraged people to move to Palestine and later to found the state of Israel. Grandma Miriam's sister decided to move to America with her husband, and the story of their arrival has passed into family legend. When their ship docked and the captain told them they had arrived in America, loudly proclaiming 'Hudson Bay', they were so excited, hoping to be greeted by the Statue of Liberty standing aloof with her torch. To their sorrow she was nowhere to be seen, which they put down to the heavy smoke puffing out of the tall factory chimneys nearby. They were walking the streets with little to their name and even less command of English when an old man saw the bewildered pair.

'Ma pets, can I help?' he asked.

All they understood was the word 'help' – it is similar in Yiddish.

'Hudson Bay?' they said hopefully.

Since the boat had anchored in Newcastle upon Tyne, on the north-east coast of England, the old man assumed he'd misheard these foreigners with their strange accent. Surely they meant the nearby Whitley Bay. He directed them to the charming seaside town, where they stopped and flourished, their Yiddish taking on a gentle Geordie lilt, though their command of English did not progress a great deal beyond 'ma pet'.

At times I feel angry at my parents for not leaving – how different our lives could have been. But they saw anti-Semitism in other countries too. Fascism was on the rise in Europe and elsewhere. Britain had Moseley and his Blackshirts. America in the 1930s was broke, with unemployment rife and the Silver Legion organization spreading hatred against the Jews. Mum and Dad had successful businesses in Ludmir and, like many in the Jewish community, simply immersed themselves in their daily lives and ignored the warning signs. They weren't alone in that. What was about to happen was inconceivable.

Chapter 2

Inklings

On 19 September 1939, three months after I was born, a red flag adorned with a hammer and sickle was proudly hoisted in Ludmir, swaying in the capricious winds from Siberia. While my brothers were still wondering what to make of their annoying baby sister, Hitler and Stalin were getting closer to a political agreement, one that would bring devastation to my home city.

A year earlier, in September 1938, Hitler had marched into Austria and had been greeted enthusiastically by euphoric crowds, like an emperor come to claim his realm. With this incredibly simple annexation, known as the Anschluss, Germany and Austria became one. Being a great gambler, Hitler thought he might just as well seize the opportunity to subsume the Sudetenland, the rich northern part of adjacent Czechoslovakia, as well.

He was very good at reading the minds of the two amateur players in Europe. Britain and France just kept schtum. The last thing they wanted was another war; they had just come up for air after the 1914–18 conflict. And so, as Hitler marched into the Sudetenland, Britain and France did not lift a finger. The gambler bluffed and won.

But in contrast to Vienna, Prague gave the Nazis no great heroes' welcome. When they moved into the country in spring of 1939, Charles Bridge was not weighed down with well-wishers throwing flowers, nor were there many bottles of Pilsner cracked open in celebration.

Having achieved political union between Germany and Austria and annexed a large slice of Czechoslovakia unopposed by the great powers of Western Europe, Hitler, flushed with these successes, figured that, since neither the British nor the French had done anything effective to stop his land grabs so far, they would remain equally passive if he now invaded Poland. But first he needed Stalin.

In August 1939 Hitler and Stalin had agreed a ten-year non-aggression treaty, the infamous Molotov–Ribbentrop Pact. The Soviet Union was meant to supply the Germans with raw materials. In return, it would receive factory-made goods, including armaments, all of the highest quality, from renowned manufacturers such as BMW, Porsche and Krupp. Russia's killing machines now sported enviably upmarket badges.

Secretly, Hitler and Stalin had also agreed to carve up eastern Europe between them, including Poland, which they would partition. On 1 September 1939, Nazi troops crossed Poland's western frontier and began their invasion. Although Britain and France declared war on Germany two days later, they did not intervene with force. The Polish military was outmatched by the German Panzer tanks, heavy artillery and Messerschmitt fighter aircraft.

Then, on 17 September 1939, the Soviet Union invaded Poland from the east. By 6 October the partition was complete: Poland had ceased to exist and Ludmir was subsumed into the Ukrainian Soviet Socialist Republic, putting us under control of the USSR and Joseph Stalin. He was a violent psychopath responsible for the Holodomor, a man-made famine which killed millions of Ukrainians between 1932 and 1933 after the authorities seized their farms and stole their grain. And yet my family, like many of the Jews and Ukrainians living in Ludmir, breathed a sigh of relief when the Red Army trucks rolled in. We were happy that the arrogant, anti-Semitic Poles were no longer in control, and hoped that the egalitarian ideology of the Bolsheviks would result in fewer restrictions in our lives.

While some people fell victim to the new Soviet regime – the larger businesses of Jews were taken away, Polish government officials lost their jobs and young men were called up to the Red Army – little changed for us and the people we knew. My parents could still run their various businesses, although my brothers' schooling was affected. From 15 November 1939, the Tarbut school they attended closed, and the instruction of Hebrew was suspended. My brothers were instead sent to a municipal school where they learned Russian alongside Jews and non-Jews. Elsewhere in Ukraine, the Soviets were said to have deported and even executed active Zionists and wealthy Jews, but I do not think that happened in Ludmir. We were too small and insignificant to draw their immediate attention.

We were more conscious of the thousands of Jews arriving in Ludmir from Poland. Overrun by Nazis, thousands of Jews fled eastward, having anticipated the fate that awaited them under the Germans. This migration turned Ludmir into an enormous refugee camp, with families torn apart after homes and livelihoods elsewhere were abandoned. Tragically, people thought that they would be safe in Ludmir under a Soviet regime.

The Jews who accurately read the situation and headed for Russia were put into Siberian labour camps, and as bad as conditions were, they were not systematically murdered there, as was the fate of Jews elsewhere. Indeed, many Jewish prisoners lived to tell their own harsh stories of survival. This was in stark contrast to the fate of most of those who fell into the hands of the likes of Hans Frank, Adolf Eichmann, Otto Wächter, Rudolf Höss and our own Erich Koch, some of the high-ranking Nazi officials who kept Albert Speer's crematoria burning at full capacity, struggling to keep up with demand, chock-a-block with human bodies, shot and piled in rows within these newly conceived extinction factories.

On 22 June 1941, by which time I was two years old, Germany invaded the Soviet Union, in a massive land offensive code-named Operation Barbarossa. It caught the Red Army completely by surprise. Despite an abundance of credible intelligence warning Stalin that a German attack was imminent, he was convinced that the next phase in German plans would be war against Great Britain. Surely, he thought, only after the Nazis had successfully overrun Britain and consolidated their power over the whole of Europe would they turn their covetous eyes towards the Soviet Union.

That Stalin ignored warnings of an imminent German invasion was not entirely irrational: it was mid-summer, and history showed that any attempt to conquer Russia so close to the start of its impenetrably harsh winters was utterly foolhardy. Waging war against one's own ally proved not only treacherous but an unbelievably ill-considered decision. Hitler had gambled yet again, believing his good luck would last, but instead his army encountered determined resistance, with huge losses, and his war chest was depleted. But while the invasion tipped the balance of the conflict, to us it also unleashed every savage excess that mankind had to offer.

A day later, Ludmir was blitzed by the Luftwaffe and the city had its first taste of what was about to be dished up far and wide. Homes were flattened and hundreds of people, particularly in the central part of the city, densely occupied by Jewish families, fell victim to the bombardment.

We somehow escaped, but bombs destroyed half of my father's bicycle shop. The Russians pulled out of the city on 24 June and, by the morning of 25 June, a formidable force of Germans, swastikas emblazoned on their armbands, knee-high black boots polished, marched into Ludmir. Over the next few weeks, my brothers would sometimes see Red Army soldiers, prisoners of war, being paraded through the streets by their captors, hollow-eyed and malnourished. They would run into the house to look for food they could give these poor men. The guards might shout and push them away but, at that time, Haim and Shalom did not fear any further reprisal. There was a POW camp nearby where the inmates were being starved, as happened to Russian prisoners throughout German territory. Haim has a particular memory of a pitiful group of soldiers dragging a cart full of dirty clothes to a public laundry and bath house, so weak they were close to collapse. He also recalls the fine feasts the German soldiers held in the stadium opposite our house, where they set out tables covered in white linen and enjoyed a hearty meal washed down with wine and beer.

Under the German occupation, a police force was formed out of local Poles and Ukrainians, and the Jewish quarter was vandalized. In early July, a Jewish council was established to coordinate life under the new authorities, which also appointed 120 men to the Jewish police. Its members were so naive that they collected valuable watches, jewellery and gold as presents to placate their new German masters. But you can't satisfy murderers. They crave your blood, not just your ransom; the more we gave, the more they killed. We were a laughing stock.

The killing started straight away. In June people were murdered in the streets, 150 Jews were killed in the courtyard of the prison and, by the end of July, a further 200 Jews had been captured and taken for slave labour never to return, with hundreds more disappearing the following month. In early August 1941, yellow patches became mandatory for Jews aged ten and over, to be displayed one on the front and one on the back of the outer coats. In mid-August bread coupons were distributed, allowing only 1 kilogram per Jewish person per week. Jewish people were regularly beaten to death by the Gestapo and the Ukraine police, and hundreds of Jews were rounded up and eliminated in September and October of 1941, including young men and 120 of the city's intelligentsia, in order to prevent any counteroffensive against the new regime.

A further demand within the first few days of German occupation was the surrender of all methods of communication; all radios were confiscated. So too were any books deemed politically or culturally unacceptable by the Third Reich, including works by leading German authors such as Brecht and Mann; they were ceremoniously piled up in the city centre and publicly burned. Jewish shops were also raided at this time, with many shop owners whisked away to undertake forced labour, never to be seen again.

My brothers no longer attended school, as one of the first acts of Erich Koch, the newly appointed Reich Commissar of Ukraine from September 1941, was to shut all schools in the country. In his opinion the young did not require knowledge, and what little that was available to them had to be taught by Germans, the pure Master Race. Anything else was of no consequence.

Koch was the most pernicious Gauleiter who ever walked the Earth. The Gestapo were under his control. His widespread cruelties were meted out across Eastern Europe, from the Baltic Sea to the Black Sea. And we became his victims.

A loyal follower of Hitler, he described himself as a 'brutal dog', and reputedly proclaimed that if ever the occasion arose where a Ukrainian of note were to share his table, he would have him shot on the spot. This was quite a high price to pay for a plate of sauerkraut and sausages. Not only did he regard himself as an exquisite host, but also as an authoritative anthropologist. He was a hard-line proponent of the Nazi ideology that the Germans were biologically and racially superior to other groups, including the Ukrainians who were destined for slave labour, while the Jews were deemed 'subhuman'. It was only a matter of time before Koch would fully unleash his programme of terror on the citizens of Ludmir.

Chapter 3

The Ghetto

It began early in 1942, the implementation of the Final Solution to the Jewish Question – the euphemistic term for the deliberate mass murder of Europe's Jews as outlined at the Wannsee Conference in January 1942. The policy was already in place of course – the conference was so that Heydrich could ensure that his SS would be in control and that the process would run smoothly. He didn't want any of the local administrators developing a conscience. Around that time, Eric Koch ordered the creation of a Jewish enclave known as a ghetto, fencing in a section of central Ludmir, near the sports stadium. Our street was not included, but on 13 April we were told to relocate and move in with other Jews within the designated area, leaving behind most of our possessions, apart from a few basics needed to survive. By now my father had been forced to abandon his various businesses to work on the railways for the Germans.

*

29

The ghetto was fenced in with three-metre-high barbed wire to prevent contact between those within it and the outside world, although main streets were left open to allow for truck transport, as guarded by policemen. Huge notices were affixed to the ghetto's barbed-wire perimeter, declaring that typhus was raging within. There was no such epidemic; the warnings were put in place merely to prevent any outside interference or attempt to bring help. The Nazis could have saved themselves the cost of the nails, however, since help from the Gentiles had no intention of coming.

In May the ghetto was subdivided into two sections: one part for people with specialist skills (where we were), the other for everyone else, which included the elderly, children, the sick and the unskilled. The inmates referred to occupants of each section as, respectively, 'the living' for the professionals and 'the dead' for the other section, which the Nazis clearly deemed superfluous and destined for liquidation.

Some people in the ghetto had built hiding places just in case. One particularly ingenious shelter was a long tunnel that had an entrance on one street and an exit on another, so that even if one opening was uncovered, those inside had time to escape from the other. Mum later told me that they were betrayed and the SS attacked from both ends, killing everyone inside.

At one point Mum had begged Dad to build a shelter for us, but my father had many German acquaintances and spoke their language perfectly and he simply did not believe that they could ever carry out such atrocities. He thought it was all a dark, passing moment in our long history; that this current

Nazi regime would not last and we would all eventually return to our normal civilized lives. My dad was a great optimist. Either he just didn't see the calamity that was unfolding right before our eyes, or else perhaps he could not allow himself to admit it.

Months later, in around August 1942, Schwarzbrot, a German engineer-surveyor, arrived to supervise the excavation of three huge pits near the village of Piatydni, six kilometres outside the city. The ghetto inmates who did the labouring were told the pits would be used to store fuel tanks for Reichsmarschall Hermann Göring's aeroplanes.

At the end of August, my grandfather came to the ghetto from his farm in Lytovezh, thirty kilometres to the south, bringing one of my mother's sisters, who was soon to give birth, and her husband. There were doctors in the ghetto and her family wanted my aunt to have the best medical care. Her tiny baby boy was born safely, and they were all with us on 1 September – a Tuesday – as we sat down for lunch. Suddenly my mother looked through the window and let out a huge scream. '*Children, we are on fire!*'

To mark the first anniversary of his reign, Erich Koch had triumphantly entered the ghetto, followed by his magnificent retinue – this included Geberit Kommissar Wilhelm Westerheide, who was in charge of our district, and his secretary (and possibly his lover), Johanna Altvater, flanked by the SS, the Gestapo and the Ukrainian police, all armed with guns. We could hear a barrage of seemingly random gun fire.

As the shooting raged, it occurred to my mother that we could hide underneath the floorboards. The ghetto house we were occupying stood on short stilts, beneath which was a gap just big enough for us to lie in. Access was through a concealed trapdoor, completely flush with the floor of the building; nobody in their wildest dreams could ever have imagined that several human beings might actually be in occupancy below.

The whole family was in hiding – Grandpa Akin and Grandma Miriam lowered themselves into that space with my parents, my brothers Haim (then ten) and Shalom (aged eight), and myself who was three. It was cramped, airless and stiflingly hot. Incredibly, my mum had the foresight to grab her satchel and put some water, bread and honey in it.

My aunt and uncle and their newborn baby had hidden up in the rafters as there wasn't enough room for so many people beneath the floorboards.

This space under the ghetto house was protected on the outside by old sheets of corrugated iron. While we were all lying there in dead silence, hardly daring to breathe, we could see between the gaps the Gestapo's boots and the hems of their long coats as they scoured every inch of the area with their huge German shepherd dogs. These dogs appeared to have more compassion than their owners since, for some reason, they couldn't or didn't sniff us out.

As we hid for our lives, the bewildered population outside were rounded up. It was said that Kommissar Westerheide stayed to ensure the whole operation was run 'smoothly'. Whether he was on horseback or on foot, he liked to carry a whip and to use it without mercy. Amid screams and gunfire, the terrified crowd clambered onto trucks as SS soldiers clubbed people with their rifle butts or shot them on the spot. Westerheide's secretary Alvater helped prod men, women and children into the trucks as if they were cattle, cracking her whip and enjoying her power.

They were taken off to Piatydni with its three pits, where Schwartzbrot had so meticulously designed the ideal mass grave. There, successive groups were told on arrival to strip and hand over any valuables. Women and girls had to unbraid their hair to prove they weren't hiding anything. Gold teeth were pulled out. And then they were forced to lie down in the pits; and when they had done so, the Einsatzgruppen (death squads) sprayed them with machine-gun fire. Then, the next group of arrivals were told to take their places on or amongst the corpses, where they too were machine-gunned to death. And this industrial conveyor-belt of murder went on and on and on and on – layer upon layer of dead bodies, mothers and fathers holding their children tight in a last act of love. Their killers were enjoying their day, with one eyewitness quoted in *Jewish Ludmir* describing them as bare-chested, hung with ammunition belts, sitting on comfortable chairs, drinking champagne and eating chocolate. This man lived in a nearby village and along with his neighbours had been conscripted to fill in the graves. They worked silently for hours, some vomiting with horror.

We heard shooting in the ghetto intermittently for about three days, after which there was a bit of a lull. Perhaps they had run out of bullets and had gone off for more. It also gave them time, while they were waiting, to loot as much as they could lay their hands on. During this pause, my father decided to climb up into the house and look for more water and bread for all of us. After he'd found some and managed to throw it down to us, my mum asked if he had seen her sister, husband and baby. In the silence that followed, it became obvious that the answer was 'No'. They had simply disappeared.

There was a hushed conversation between Mum and Dad. Suddenly we heard approaching footsteps. Dad said to Mum, 'Save the children.' That was the last time we heard his voice. He shut the trapdoor instantly and moved away, not wanting to risk being seen as he squeezed in. My brave, idealistic father sacrificed his life to ensure we were not discovered.

That single noise, that slamming of the trapdoor, shattered the lives of my grandmother, who had just lost her son, my mother who was now widowed in her early thirties and us children who had just lost our father. Three generations, bereaved in an instant.

We never found out exactly what happened to Dad. He was taken away and became one of the thousands from our city who were shot, whose death was not recorded, who probably lies in a mass grave at Piatydni.

A few days later, Grandad left. Despite Mum begging him to stay, he felt he had to make his way back to his village on foot, anxious to return home to Grandma Hannah. If he did get to the farmhouse, there would have been no one to greet him. Grandma Hannah had been taken away, with other Jewish villagers, and shot at a place called Ivanich. We later heard from eyewitnesses that Grandpa spent the night hiding in a tree in one of his fields, where the sheaves were waiting to be collected by the gleaners. He was captured and killed the following day. Some of his neighbours, who were Christians, buried him on the land he'd loved.

I was terrified by all of this: the weeping, the craving for water, the hunger, the sound of the Gestapo's boots stamping across the floorboards above, the smashing of glass and the ear-shattering anger of the guns. Throughout our time in hiding there, at night, Mum would crawl out and head into the fields. She owned some land nearby in partnership with Grandpa Akin which they used to grow vegetables to sell so she knew the area. She would gather whatever she could find – some onions, maize, beetroot and green tomatoes. In the darkness, of course, she couldn't see if they were ripe or not. Curiously, I developed a lifelong passion for green tomatoes; indeed, for a long time I had no idea they were actually meant to be red. These were tomatoes far beyond price. My mother could have paid with her life if she had been caught. From as early as I can remember, she was so fearless and determined.

After fifteen days of their raging firestorm, '*Aktion*' ('action') as the Germans called it, rather than the more correct term 'pogrom', the guns finally fell silent on 15 September 1942. Unknown to us then, this silence signalled the end of this first pogrom, during which Schwartzbrot's methodically thought-out pits in Piatydni began to reach their full, prearranged capacity, with the discarded corpses of around 15,000 men, women and children. These same pits that we had casually been told were intended for fuel for Göring's planes. 15,000 people, ended. Without a hint of mercy.

In the silence that followed, we tentatively made our way

out from underneath our floorboards, dazed and disoriented, and emerged into a numbing new landscape, a shattered carnage, fashioned by men who had transformed themselves into cold-blooded, pitiless savages. We hesitantly walked amongst the shattered glass and debris that had once been our ghetto house.

Two Ukraine policemen, armed with huge clubs spiked with menacing, razor-sharp metal, called out to us to leave immediately – '*Chipko, chipko*,' (Quick, quick) – and to go through the barbed wire that led into the smaller ghetto. Here, the remaining people – around 4,000 – were to stay.

The Ukraine police were not allowed to bear firearms themselves. The Germans didn't trust them in case they turned their weapons on them, though there was never really the slightest prospect of that happening. Not only was this a golden opportunity for them to plunder but, after eighteen months of Stalin's repression, they regarded the Germans as their liberators.

The threatening tone of the policemen's orders did not allow us adequate time to say any last farewell to this place that had been our home for about eight months. As we arrived at the forbidding, three-metre-high wall of barbed wire which we all had to negotiate in order to go to the other side where the second ghetto was located, Grandma found it difficult to get through and had to be helped by Haim. Shalom caught his coat on the barbs when it was his turn, so Mum held me in one hand and tried to untangle him with her other, which was taking time to do. And throughout this highly tense ordeal, loud voices threatened and screamed in Ukrainian, '*Chipko, chipko*.'

Just then, a German SS officer in his imposing uniform,

armed with a pistol in his holster, approached us with a pleasant smile on his face, untangled my brother and said to Mum, 'What a beautiful boy.' Mum was stunned. She was certain he was going to unleash an explosion of bullets, and yet he inexplicably came to help. Only yesterday, he would have participated in the killing of thousands of people; and now here he was helping a young boy to free himself from barbed wire.

When I think about this incident – as I have almost daily for eighty years – I can never understand what inspired such mercy in an officer in the SS, an organization dedicated to the destruction of a whole race, of which we were defenceless members. It seems to represent the madness of the time and the illogic of mankind.

It was in the second ghetto that Grandma Miriam discovered she had lost not one but two sons in the pogrom. Her youngest boy Joel had been killed too. And when Mum went looking for her family members who had been in the ghetto – her grandmother, brothers, sisters, aunts, uncles and cousins – she found that the entire Akin family had been eradicated apart from one cousin, Rachel. Grandma could barely speak. She sat in a corner of our tiny new house and wrapped herself in her old shawl, unable to face the world. Mum was broken. She'd just lost Dad, who was a part of herself. They had been inseparable in work and life. What kept her functioning was her strength of spirit and Dad's last words, his plea that she must save the children.

Chapter 4

A Chance to Live

Once we entered the second ghetto, it was absolutely vital for Mum to obtain a blue work permit. Anyone without one was considered to be illegal, and could be taken out at any time and shot. In the first ghetto, Dad had had a blue work permit, although the safety provided by such a document had been illusory.

Life in this 'ghetto for the dead' – if one could call it life – was overseen by two men who had power over us: Leib Kudysh, who was the head of the Jewish Council, and Zavidovich, the head of the Jewish police. Soon after our arrival, Mum went to the council to ask for a blue permit, but they refused. Most of the allocated passes had already been given out to their own families and their cronies. And in any case, the last person they would ever grant one to was a woman.

Mum already knew Kudysh, who had been a barber in Ludmir before the war, and also a member of the synagogue that my parents attended. She appealed to him, pointing out that she had lost her husband and now had to care for her old mother-in-law and three small children. Kudysh seemed unmoved by this. Since he had been charging money for permits, earning himself a tidy sum, he was presumably reluctant to give one away for free. Mum added that no one in the ghetto would last much longer, not even him. Still he said no. But if he was the immovable object, Mum was the unstoppable force. She later said that she'd told him: 'Your "no" is of very little importance to me. I'm not leaving until I have a pass. I want to give my children a chance to live, if only for a very short time.' He grumbled and prevaricated and argued but, finally, despite his apparently unshakeable reluctance, Mum emerged with the essential document.

Safely authorized, Mum could now go off with the working men on the lorries while Grandma Miriam kept us children safe. Her first job involved digging the fields, supervised by the Wehrmacht. When the sun started to go down, the soldiers would make themselves invisible to give the labourers a chance to hide a few potatoes and beetroot. They even looked a bit embarrassed to see them slaving away.

Our house (more of a hovel really) had a small window, and every afternoon Grandma Miriam and my brothers would look out for Mum's return, hoping that hidden on her person would be something we could eat. Hunger was a constant gnawing ache. That was how we lived. And during this time, Mum made a little linen bag in which she always kept the crucial permit hanging round her neck.

Later, when she was cleaning the Gestapo and SS barracks, Mum asked the guard there to give her some cloth so she could wash the windows. He grabbed her by her hair and pulled out a handful. Opening the palm of his hand he said, 'This is what you clean the windows with.'

One of the additional benefits of holding a work permit issued by the Jewish Council was that anyone else who happened to occupy the same room as someone who possessed one – and this could involve as many as ten or more – was also regarded as being covered by whatever safety it conferred and, therefore, these others were also hypothetically exempt from being instantly removed for execution. Although this offered only temporary protection for them (and us), it at least provided some with a chance to live and breathe another day.

Mum used this curious loophole to help save others whenever and wherever possible. Our little hovel was a temporary sanctuary.

In an effort to ingratiate themselves with their oppressors, Jewish Council members built a jetty near the ghetto on the River Luha, so that the German command could fish and go kayaking in my dad's kayaks. They also collected gold, which they used to decorate a lavish special peaked cap for Wilhelm Westerheide. Why didn't Kudysh use the money to buy a gun and shoot Westerheide? There would have been reprisals but our lives were transitory in any case. At least it would have showed he had some pride.

On the anniversary of the first pogrom, when people from the ghetto had permission to go to Piatydni to pray for the many thousands who had been exterminated, Kudish organized a big party for his family and friends to celebrate his silver wedding anniversary. Needless to say, we were not invited.

The Jewish Council and the Jewish police had a great deal to answer for with regard to the fates of so many of the Nazis' victims. They made up lists of 'illegal' people, who didn't possess work permits to give to Westerheide. These people were to be taken out of the ghetto and disposed of – and by now, there was no doubt about the fate they would meet. The hands of Kudish and Zavidovich were awash with the blood of their own people and their duplicity had no limits.

Zavidovich was unusually evil, even by the standards of the time. He would get hold of young boys, including my brothers, and beat them with heavy straps of leather, even making them lower their pants. Only when he saw blood begin to flow would he let them go. Their hands were so sore they could hardly lift their trousers. Mum had known the family that spawned this sadist. They too had been members of our synagogue before the invasion.

As children were taboo in the ghetto, it was very difficult to complain. Nevertheless, when Mum heard what had been done to Haim and Shalom, she gathered her strength, went to the Jewish police station and demanded to talk to Zavidovich, who appeared in his police uniform with a Star of David on its armband. Mum later said that she'd given it to him straight, that she was ashamed of his actions as a Jew and as a human being: wasn't what the Germans were inflicting on us enough, without the victims' connivance and cooperation?

Zavidovich told her to come to his office and ordered her to lie on the bench, face down. He took out a thick belt and beat her until he saw blood coming from her back, and he told her this was only a starter because of her complaining. Poor Mum. She suffered so much for sticking up for her children, but she was proud. She thought that both she and he would survive, and that in the event she would be able to look the world in the eye, whereas he would never be able to.

In the ghetto, such creatures held the power of life and death over us all. Their brutality was a way to placate the Germans and save their own skin. And if any one of us complained, all they had to do was report us as illegals and we would not see the following sabbath.

On 14 November 1942, in the middle of the night, the second pogrom erupted. The shooting started again, and they began rounding people up and taking them off to the city prison. By this time, I was three and a half years old.

My grandmother, my two brothers, my mum and I were hiding in a shelter along with some other Jews, a secret space in the rafters of a house. I don't know how we got there; I think we just tagged along with a group. Everyone sat in tense silence, ears straining to hear any sound that meant our hunters were near. I was frightened and I started to yell. A young man who was with us in the shelter grabbed me out of Mum's arms, produced a big leather belt and put it round my neck to strangle me. If the Germans had heard my crying, they would have discovered us all. Mum pleaded with him to release his grip on me, and he reluctantly took the belt from my throat. She picked me up and stood to leave the shelter. She begged Grandma and the boys to stay, but they all declined and came out with us. That harrowing moment has stayed with me ever since but unfortunately such experiences were not unique. I have read accounts of crying infants in shelters having their faces covered with a pillow and being accidentally smothered. Sometimes the death of a baby was not a mistake. Such extreme situations bring out the worst in people.

With no time to waste, Mum told us to get under the beds in the house. Shalom slipped under one with Grandma, Haim found his own and Mum and I crawled under another, where she held me in her arms and we curled up, making ourselves as small as possible. And so we waited, hearts pounding, in our flimsy hiding places. Suddenly, Mum heard a scuffle from one of the other rooms, followed by footsteps coming closer and then we were being dragged out. Haim was found last. The guards forced us onto the street where we joined people being taken at gunpoint to the prison yard where they were gathering those who'd survived the first pogrom, around 4,000 people.

In all the mayhem, Haim was separated from us. I later learned that he'd been spotted by a Ukrainian who knew my dad and ran a shop that sold feathers for pillows and eiderdowns. He took Haim in and told him to hide in his mountain of feathers until the coast was clear. Later, he gave my brother a hearty meal and told him he was welcome to stay for as long as necessary, even until the war was over. Haim thanked him but said, 'I must rejoin my mother and the rest.' He was just eleven years old.

After he left the shop, he was caught and escorted to the prison yard where we were all confined. When he told Mum what had happened, she asked him why he hadn't accepted the kind man's offer. To which Haim replied: 'What was the point, if you were all going to your deaths?' That is very typical of my big brother.

We learned afterwards that the shelter in which we had been hiding, and where my fate was so nearly sealed, had been discovered by Westerheide, and every single person inside had been murdered on the spot.

This second '*Aktion*' was mainly conducted by Westerheide, the Gestapo and the Ukraine police. I am lucky that the reality of our situation was lost on me. My mother knew what was to come so that, when the guards tried to separate her from my brothers, as women and men were being loaded onto separate trucks, she fought to keep the boys with her. Holding them to her, she desperately tried to reason with the guard.

'Look, we're going to be killed anyway, but I would like to undress my children with my own hands before going in the pit. I want them to be with me.'

The guard just laughed at her. 'You're stupid, you're going to meet them there anyway.'

How cruel he was, this man who could have been a neighbour or one of Dad's customers in the past. Mum didn't shout at him, knowing that would lead to instant death; instead, she tried to persuade him. Trucks full of people left while Mum was arguing, and more came. The guards were dividing people into three rows of eleven per row. Amidst the hunger, the snow underfoot and the despair, the cries for help became agonizing and overwhelming. Every one of us was in a queue to be taken away to the killing fields of Piatydni. We were to be loaded onto a truck, the maximum capacity of which was thirty-three human beings.

As our turn to board the truck got closer, we all stood in a row to be counted. As fate would have it, my grandmother was number thirty-three, I was number thirty-four, Mum was number thirty-five and the boys were numbers thirty-six and thirty-seven. The meticulous German guard who kept the books indicated a separation between Grandma and me. She, as number thirty-three, was the last to join those queueing ahead of us on the truck waiting to carry them all away.

I screamed for Grandma when she was torn away from me and roughly shoved onto the truck. How could any mother's son be so brutal to an old woman?

As we waited our turn for the next empty vehicle to take us on our journey to death Mum took the little bundle of coins and jewellery that she had saved, which she kept hidden under her skirt in a little bag tied to elastic. She quickly crouched and dropped it down a drain. She would have been in trouble if she had been seen, but she refused to hand it over to the Germans or Ukrainians.

In the prison building itself, there were a lot of non-Jewish political detainees. One of them, who was looking out of a window, recognized Mum and shouted to her: 'Mrs Fischmann, what are you doing here? With all your connections and wealth? Why didn't you escape?' Mum said, 'I am here with all the others.' The prisoner threw some bread and garlic out to us. We children were so hungry that even at such a terrible moment we grabbed the bread and, with hands made clumsy by the the cold, we pulled it into chunks to eat.

While all this calamity was unfolding, standing in that freezing prison yard we noticed Uncle Hirsch, my father's brother, running in our direction, accompanied by a high-ranking German officer from the Wehrmacht. As soon as my uncle found us in the queue, he asked where his mother was. As he looked around, he saw her aboard the truck; but it was too late to get her removed.

The officer and my uncle were there to take us out of the prison. There was a lot of quarrelling between the officer and the guards. 'Why should they go out?' they demanded. But the officer was very firm and gave a strict order to release us. It is fortunate that Westerhiede was not there as the Wehrmacht did not have any sway with the SS. The officer and my uncle took us away, and we were escorted back to the ghetto. Uncle Hirsch was working in a factory where that humane officer was in charge, and the two had an understanding. Hirsch told him that we were his family and the brave officer came and saved us. His actions were not without risk – to help a Jew could result in a court martial, or perhaps dispatch to the meatgrinder that was the Eastern Front and likely death. That moment was almost beyond our comprehension; it was a miraculous event that I still cannot grasp. And if my mother had not argued with the ignorant guards over my brothers, we would have been on an earlier truck and gone before Hirsch could arrive. On such small consequences hung the difference between life and death.

For this second '*Aktion*', in which 4,000 Jews were murdered, these butchers received 80,000 German marks. Or at least, that's the amount they were due to have been paid. But in keeping with German precision, the figure had to be recalculated. Since we four were ultimately not part of the mass killing, 80 marks had to be deducted from the total payment.

Being just a very young child throughout this period, I was less aware than I would otherwise have been of the catastrophic, pressing events that were now unfolding in rapid succession. Instead, my abiding memory throughout this time was the feeling of being constantly cold. Freezing. In the prison yard, I had had no notion that we were queuing up to be taken to our deaths. I just knew that my hands were icy and my coat was too small and my frozen fingers were not supple enough to secure my buttons in their buttonholes. It was mid-November; and my greatest difficulty was this constant, intolerable raw cold.

In my distress, I asked Mum to do the buttons up for me. This at a time when Mum was acutely aware that we were waiting in line for our deaths.

For all her steadfastness and courage in negotiating and ensuring the survival of her children throughout this nightmare, on that day, waiting for the truck to take us all off to our deaths . . . that day, she told me years later, was the one time her resolve had cracked.

In that single moment, when her frozen child asked her to button up her ill-fitting coat for whatever imagined comfort it might have provided, on that day, in that moment, waiting for the conveyance that was on its way to take us all off to be machine-gunned to death within the next half-hour or so, Mum's only thought was: What does it matter if my child catches a cold?

Her reaction was totally natural and yet it must have been one of the most painful memories for my poor mum as it weighed so heavily on her mind that, years later, she would still dwell on it.

Chapter 5

Borrowed Time

There were so few of us left now, just five or six hundred people who were mostly slave labour and still useful to the Nazi regime. We were moved again into our third and even smaller ghetto in the south-west of the city, where my brothers and I were amongst a handful of surviving children. We were obvious targets now.

By spring 1943, we had a hunch that the Germans were taking a beating from the Soviets and sustaining heavy losses. We didn't have any updated news, of course, since all our means of communication had been confiscated. There were no radios. The only way for us to know how things stood was to interpret the actions of the Germans themselves. When they were losing a battle, as retribution they would pick up a few hundred Jews from the ghetto and beat them to death or shoot them, depending on which method gave them the biggest kick. But equally, even when they made gains in battle, they would still select a few dozen Jews and shoot them just for the thrill of it.

The most devastating loss suffered to date by the hitherto

invincible German army was at Stalingrad (August 1942–February 1943). A lot of the credit goes to the Red Army's charismatic General Zhukov, a lucky commander who was helped by the fact the German army was trying to fight in one of the most ferocious winters in living memory. There was a German SS officer named Keller who was in charge of the police station in the ghetto, and he strutted about with a terrifying German shepherd dog named Stalin. This dog was so vicious, I have no doubt he was the Gauleiter of the dog kingdom. But when news of the Stalingrad defeat reached him, the inconsolable Keller shot the dog dead. And from this patriotic act, we were able to work out that the Soviets were beating the Germans and that our captors were on the back foot.

This defeat turned the tide of the war, but it wasn't going to help us. After the second pogrom, it became clear that the complete annihilation of all of us was near. When Erich Koch next visited the ghetto, along with Gebietskommisar Westerheide, my mother recognized that the door would almost certainly then be closing for good on any further chances for our survival. She immediately put her mind to finding a way out.

Mum knew that our cousin Rachel (her father and Grandpa Akin were brothers) had survived, the only member of our extended family of seventy-eight to do so. At that time, she was alone, having lost her husband and her only son aged six in the first pogrom. Somehow she had managed to obtain fake Aryan documents. I have no idea how. She wasn't well known in our city since she came from a different part of the country, so she could easily mingle amongst the crowds and remain unnoticed. She lived outside the ghetto.

The other member of my family who was still alive was Uncle Hirsch, who had rescued us all from the prison in the second pogrom. He had by this time lost his mother, his wife and his two children.

Mum arranged to meet up with Rachel and Hirsch, who suggested that Haim should join him in an attempt to flee. He and a few other men from the ghetto were planning to escape to the marshlands of Pinsk– a very hostile terrain of forests and wetlands. Polish and Soviet partisans were sheltering there, as well as some Jews who had escaped the Łachwa ghetto in Poland (now Lakhva, Belarus). There Uncle Hirsh and the other men hoped to stay safely until the end of the war. That would have been one brother taken care of and, it was hoped, one who would live. Shalom could go with Rachel, who would hide him. (He was the same age as the son she had lost, and she had always felt close to him.) So, that would leave my mother and me by ourselves. It was thought that, being just the two of us, it would give us a far better chance of survival. I was the weakest link.

It sounded a sensible plan; with luck, perhaps one of us would survive to tell the story: 'Once, there was a woman with three children . . .'

Mum was never one to make impulsive decisions and she wasn't a percentage player. On the surface it all made sense, but she would need some time to mull it over. The following week, Mum met up with Rachel and they discussed the plan further. Mum thought it would be too dangerous for Rachel to take on Shalom since our family was quite well known in Ludmir. There was always the chance that some Polish or Ukrainian resident would recognize a Jewish boy and denounce them both to the police. And there was always the strong possibility that she might, at any time, be arbitrarily stopped by some suspicious, bloodthirsty German. He would just need to order the boy to lower his trousers to see if he was circumcised and that alone would mean death. The Poles, Ukrainians and Germans were always on the lookout for Jews who were out of the ghetto. They were such easy targets.

Mum wondered if there was a Christian family that might be persuaded to take us in; although the Germans had taken most of her wealth, she still had a small amount hidden away and would of course pay them for their kindness. And if the hosts were farmers, she could work for them too; she was raised a country girl. Then suddenly she had an idea: before the war, a man named Ribke used to come to the family bicycle shop to buy spare parts. It was even possible that he and my father had gone racing together. Ribke was an ardent Ukrainian nationalist who sought independence for his homeland. He wanted the Germans gone, but if his country was then taken over by the Russians, whom he disliked every bit as much, there was no doubt that they would regard him as a collaborator. As my mum saw it, what better way could there possibly be for a Ukrainian to demonstrate to a Russian that he was anti-Nazi than for him to have saved a Jewish family from the Holocaust? Mum must also have known that she could trust Ribke with our safety and with Rachel's.

Rachel listened carefully to Mum and said she would get in touch with Ribke to see if he could help. He also had a lot of contacts of his own and might come up with some other idea that would help us.

The two cousins parted and Mum went back to the ghetto. Even such a simple meeting as this presented extraordinary dangers for Mum. Ironically, being in the ghetto was less risky than just walking in the city streets.

But this ever-present danger was not the only reason Mum had asked Rachel to contact Ribke instead of going to see him herself. Being visited by a woman wearing a coat emblazoned with a yellow patch must surely also taint him, adding its own obvious risks. Caught in the prying eyes of passing Germans, or even local people, such a meeting could easily have marked him out as yet another enemy of the Third Reich. No. Rachel, with her false papers and Aryan looks, was far better placed to accomplish such a task without arousing suspicion.

On the way back to the ghetto, Mum would buy food from people she knew. Afterwards, she would occasionally visit Stacha, a Polish woman who had been her dressmaker and now sometimes looked after the boys when Mum felt it was too risky for them to be in the ghetto. On such days, the boys couldn't wait to see Mum. Whenever they guessed she was near they would crawl out from their hiding place in Stacha's house and hover next to the curtains to see if she was coming. As soon as they caught a glimpse of her, they would surreptitiously twitch the curtains – their signal that they were still alive.

Mum was constantly in a terrible state of fear. Just walking to Stacha's was in no way risk-free. If ever she opened the door and the boys hadn't moved the curtain, she dreaded that they might have been taken away, never to be seen again. They were regularly kept behind a cupboard, which was placed across the corner of the room, and forbidden to speak in case somebody came to the house and heard their voices. As a result of such lengthy confinements, my middle brother actually lost his voice for a time and couldn't talk at all. Mum was absolutely devastated by this, thinking he might remain dumb for the rest of his life. There was no way I could be trusted to keep silent, so I was left in the ghetto. I assume Mum asked one of the women she knew to look after me. I don't remember but as soon as I started writing this I had to stop. My hand refused to move, fear swept through me and I struggled to catch my breath. I felt like a toddler, left alone with a stranger, having to hide her fear.

Each time Mum returned to the ghetto after seeing the boys, there was a real risk it would be her very last walk. Such were the constant agonizing perils of trying to negotiate a path unnoticed through this jungle of hostile Germans, Poles and Ukrainians. My mother clearly had nerves of steel.

When she could, Mum remunerated Stacha for the risk she was taking; she paid her by giving her cloth she'd bought from people in the ghetto, who had stashed it away from the Germans and now wanted to sell it. For this was Stacha's lifeline: such commodities were at a premium and particularly hard to come by in Ludmir, since most of the merchants dealing in such goods had been wiped out.

Whenever she was smuggling the cloth from the ghetto, she would wrap it around her body and wear her large beige trench coat. Mum was very slim and of above average height, so she didn't look out of place in such a wrapping. Her Achilles heel, however, was her feet. Mum had big feet (size 40), but whenever she went to buy shoes, she always insisted she was a 39. She never admitted her true size and wondered why her feet were sore. When people noticed that she always seemed to be one step ahead of everyone else, she would say, "It's because I have big feet."'

Her meetings with my Uncle Hirsch were overshadowed by the overwhelming sorrow they felt at the loss of their loved ones who had perished at the hands of such craven sadists. Understandably, at this time, Mum was in a state of utter despair. She told him about her plan to approach Ribke and said:

'If I should survive this tragedy and one of my children didn't, my life wouldn't be worth living. I would never forgive myself. And my vow to your brother to "save the children" would have been in vain.'

Hirsch tried to encourage her, saying that if she could get through to Ribke then she had every chance of finding shelter for the rest of the war.

Now four years old, understandably my opinion was deemed irrelevant whenever plans for our survival were discussed. The truth was, I was just a hanger-on. In fact, I always seemed to be the problem, often weeping, confused about what was going on. It was winter; my shoes were too small and so full of holes that my feet were drowning in pools of water; my old coat was two sizes too small. I could never button it up, not just because the two sides barely met, but because my hands were frozen and I couldn't fit the button through its hole. I was hanging on to a woman who was grief-stricken, tormented by the past and fighting against the surrounding bleakness now. Most of all, I missed my dad and Grandma and couldn't understand why they weren't with us. I was hungry and too frightened to walk the ghetto streets, which were lined with the bodies of the dead, their eyes wide open as if asking, 'Why?' The fear in a child living in the midst of such inexplicable adversity was understandable. I was just thoroughly overwhelmed by the situation. I was so young, so vocal; I would not have made a reliable co-escapee. I was a child with no childhood.

A rumour was now spreading that 'the great and the good' of the High Command and the Gestapo planned to pay another visit to the ghetto in order to wish us well and use the opportunity to shoot a few hundred more of us in passing. As soon as this alarming news reached Mum, she made plans to get the boys out of sight and over to Stacha's until the hunters had finished their cull. Mum never took the two boys together, it was always one at a time, in case they were caught. That way, at least there would be one left. Being a local, she knew the city like the back of her hand. In fact, some of the land she crossed had actually belonged to her. And she also knew how to dodge the hunters in order not to become one of their trophies.

The first brother she delivered to Stacha was Shalom, who was immediately secreted behind a cupboard. The next day, Mum left the ghetto with Haim at her side. When they were halfway to Stacha's, they passed a young Polish lad. It is hard to take in how deep the hatred for Jews was, being embedded even in children. Recognizing my brother, he went straight to a Polish policeman to tell him he'd seen a Jewish woman and her son who had come from the ghetto. The policeman ran out of his house, loading his gun, and began shouting to Mum and Haim to come back. Mum paid no attention and started walking faster. Then the policeman began to whistle loudly and yelled for them to return. If they didn't, he said he was going to shoot.

Mum realized that this time there wouldn't be a next time. This was the last she was to see of Haim. She told him to run to Stacha's and turned to the policeman to meet her end. The policeman was roaring with rage and demanded to know why she was out of the ghetto, then he made her walk into an orchard (it might even have been her own father's orchard). Once there, he held his pistol to her head. Before he could pull the trigger, an old German Wehrmacht officer, who was passing by and had witnessed what was going on, called out to the Pole to stop.

'What has she done to you?' he asked.

'She is Jewish and has no right to walk outside the ghetto,' the Pole replied, loathing in his voice. The officer told him he'd better put down the gun.

'It would be a good idea to leave the killing to us Germans,' he said.

The Pole raged at this officer for robbing him of the opportunity to kill this Jewish woman. Perhaps he was thinking of his 20 marks reward or perhaps his hatred for Jews meant he was simply furious he lost the chance to add another victim to his long list. He certainly wasn't going to just let Mum go without inflicting some pain. He struck her head so fiercely with the handle of his pistol that she fell to the ground and lost consciousness. The German officer waited by her side while she came to and gradually regained some strength, and eventually asked her to get up slowly if she could. Once she was on her feet, he escorted her back to the ghetto gates. He didn't exchange many words with her, although Mum spoke German quite well. The only thing he said to her was that he was ashamed of what was being inflicted upon her people.

'But one day, history will judge us,' he said.

In the midst of all this darkness, acts of humanity could still shine forth. Mum never forgot him.

When Mum reached the entrance to the ghetto, Haim was standing there, banging his head against the iron gates, shouting and weeping: 'I lost my father and now I've lost my mother.' When he saw Mum, he couldn't believe that she was still alive. He was certain that she had gone to join our father. He was in such a state, he couldn't take in what she was telling him. He kept hugging her to make sure he was not hallucinating.

When they went back to the hovel in the ghetto, they sat on the iron bed and Haim told Mum that when he got to Stacha's she had grabbed her black lace mantilla and rushed to church, where she was planning to light some candles and beg Holy Mary to save her friend.

'Why didn't you stay with Stacha?' Mum asked.

He said he had told Stacha that he needed to get back to the ghetto to take care of his sister.

Erich Koch's next visit to the ghetto, as expected, included many of the great dignitaries of the Third Reich as well as his usual entourage. Westerheide, the Kommissar in charge of our ghetto, was there with his secretary, Johanna Altvater, a sadist who couldn't bear the sight of small children. Various eyewitnesses saw Altvater inflict terrible violence on the children of the ghetto, luring them with sweets before then shooting into their open mouths with a small pistol by her side. She was said also to have snatched a toddler from his mother's arms, grabbing him by his legs and then smashing his head against a wall, and while visiting a makeshift hospital, she threw bedridden children from balconies to their deaths.

All of this retinue, including Keller, came to see how the ghetto was 'flourishing', no doubt while calculating how many more bullets would be required to achieve the successful completion of the Führer's master plan.

As soon as we heard that Koch was on his way, the boys rushed over to Stacha's. In order to ensure that I escaped the Gauleiter's notice, Mum thought it would be safer to put me out of sight on top of a cupboard. It was a good plan, but unfortunately the grand cortège came riding by on horses, giving them a higher vantage point than expected. They all glanced through the small window of our hovel as they passed and spotted me sitting there on my perch. For some reason, they didn't like the look of me. Mum heard them make some remark that suggested I wouldn't be around for much longer. To this day, I can't imagine what went through their minds. Perhaps my blonde pigtails weren't properly plaited.

Mum was in an agony of apprehension until night fell and she felt she could leave the ghetto. She took me through the barbed wire and hurried along the dark city streets to Stacha's. Since I couldn't be trusted to keep silent, I was put in a cot with a crucifix around my neck. Being blonde and blue-eyed, I just might pass as a relative if the police arrived at the house. I probably slept well on my comfortable mattress, tucked up under a blanket, compared to Mum and my brothers who spent the night in Stacha's dark cubbyhole, covered in rolls of cloth, a flimsy barrier against any determined search.

Once back in the ghetto, it soon become apparent that Haim was no longer very enthusiastic about staying at Stacha's. It wasn't that Stacha was in any way unkind to the boys; in fact, she was great. The problem was her husband, who was an alcoholic. All the money she earned from our mum actually went on his drink.

And it wasn't just the money he got through; there were other problems. There was always the danger that whenever he was drunk, or if they'd quarrelled, he might blurt out in a rage that Stacha hid Jewish children. Mum knew this was far too dangerous a situation to continue. Stacha was an absolute angel, who risked a lot to help us; but it was almost certain she would eventually be returning to Poland in any case. So, once Mum had heard about this dreadful state of affairs from Haim, she said that, after Koch's visit, the boys would never be taken there again. There would be a new plan. And that plan could only mean escape.

Chapter 6

Somewhere . . . Elsewhere

I was never quite clear how we knew Mrs Skovronsky, who was Polish. Looking back, I decided that her husband probably worked for my dad before the war. The important thing about her is that my parents trusted her and her husband. For all his optimism about the situation, Dad had nevertheless had the foresight to give the Skovronskys some jewellery and Russian gold sovereigns for safe keeping. If Mum was going to plan an escape, she would need these as she had nothing else left, having thrown the rest of her money down the prison yard drain. And so, once again, she braved the journey out of the ghetto. Mrs Skovronsky was stunned but delighted to see Mum. Mum told her about Koch's visit and said she could see that the inhabitants in the ghetto were now in grave and imminent danger. This must have been in November 1943.

From there, Mum met up with Rachel. Even now, I am astonished by Mum's courage, how she managed to dodge all the terrifying dangers that lurked along the way. She had many a narrow escape.

Rachel told Mum that she had seen Ribke. He remembered us well and was astonished that we were among the few still alive, but devastated to learn that my father was no longer here. Ribke was going to make a trip to visit his uncle in a village named Biscobich, about fifteen kilometres south-west of Ludmir, and would try to persuade his uncle to take us all in. At first, he was not going to tell him that it would be a woman with three small children, but rather a husband and wife who would work for him on the farm. Ribke was going to let Rachel know the outcome of the visit in a few days' time, and he hoped very much that he would be successful.

After a few anxious days, Mum met up again with Rachel, who had some possibly good news. She said that Ribke's uncle and aunt, the Yakimchuks, would be coming at the end of the week to see if these new recruits would satisfy their specifications and make them rich. Rachel said we must be ready to meet them and, hopefully, they would take us in. We were sure our perfect CVs would fit their requirements. Mum was over the moon with this tiny glimmer of hope.

The following night, we left the ghetto for the last time. It hadn't taken very much preparation for this new journey, since nearly all our possessions had been seized by the SS and the Gestapo. We always slept with our clothes and shoes on, ready to flee at a moment's notice. We quickly made our way to Ribke's through the wires and, as usual, I was the slowcoach. I couldn't keep up with my brothers; my coat was caught on the wire, meaning yet another rip was added to the fabric.

We arrived frightened and exhausted. Mr and Mrs Yakimchuk appeared soon after us, and Ribke showed them into a

different room from the one where we were waiting for them.
I later learned that Mr Yakimchuk then asked: 'Where are my
fine recruits? Where are the husband and wife?' Ribke was
slightly hesitant at first. Then he started to explain that it
wasn't quite as straightforward as he had originally suggested.
He mumbled, 'It is a woman with a family.' He wasn't quite
ready to lay all his cards on the table just yet, or to mention
that only the mother was older than twelve.

A huge row erupted. Mr Yakimchuk reproached his nephew
for lying, then protested that if he took on such a family, he
would not only endanger himself and his wife but also their
entire village. To make matters worse, his own daughter, Paraska, was gravely ill at home and his son, Ivan, had been
recruited by the Germans to help them dig fortifications. His
whole neighbourhood was teeming with Ukrainian militia who
were cooperating with the SS and the Gestapo to root out
Russians and Jews, and any locals harbouring them would be
shot. If he did what was now being asked of him, he concluded,
not unreasonably, 'I might just as well put a rope around my
neck – or better still, round yours.'

Ribke tried to calm Mr Yakimchuk down, suggesting that
he was probably tired from his journey and might see things
differently after a rest. This did not land well, but then Mrs
Yakimchuk joined in, telling her husband not to be so opposed
to the idea and that he should reserve judgement until he actually met the people seeking refuge.

Mr Yakimchuk then really lost his temper with her, demanding to know what the village priest would think if he knew that
she was proposing to bring back such a dangerous bunch. We

later learned that Mrs Yakimchuk was only too familiar with her husband's tirades against the Orthodox Church, whose members he liked to denounce as hypocrites who were pious on Sundays while spending the other six days of the week helping Nazis throw Jews down wells.

Leave the priest to me, she told him. But Mr Yakimchuk was unconvinced, demanding: 'Can't you see any further than your stupid godly fantasies?'

Ribke then suggested that it was time for them to meet their prospective lodgers. At this point Mr Yakimchuk declared that he didn't want to meet anyone, and walked out of the house in a huff. In the yard he sat on his wagon and spoke a few words of wisdom to his horse. (We became familiar with this odd trait: in times of adversity or uncertainty, Mr Yakimchuk would always talk things over with his equine confidant.) Evidently, on this occasion, the horse did nothing to allay his initial fear that taking on these people would bring calamity to everyone involved in the scheme as well as many others who were not.

Eventually when he came back into the house, the four of us were standing there in a line, as if on parade. He took one look, burst out laughing and turned to Ribke.

'Have you taken leave of your senses? You think that this lot will work on my farm and make me rich? Is this some kind of sick joke?'

Mum turned to Mr Yakimchuk and addressed him in Ukrainian, which she spoke quite well, although her main languages – apart from Yiddish – were Russian and Polish. She knew exactly how to play on the farmer's emotional heart strings, with her background in a farming family.

She told him that her father had had dealings with many Ukrainian farmers. He would buy their crops by the acreage, tell them what grain he was interested in and pay in advance. It was a bit of a gamble to know if it would be a good yield or a bad one, but, on the whole, the crops were good as the land was so fertile. Having worked alongside her father, she explained she had bought fields of wheat and barley and knew the business inside out, and that they had made good money in the process. This was Mum's last throw of the dice, using all her powers of persuasion. But still, Mr Yakimchuk said, '*Nyet.*'

The old man was now nearing his wits' end. He was adamant that he was not going to put his family at risk and that his beloved half-lame horse would not be taking us on the scenic route back through the countryside to Biscobich. Ribke helped him to another drink, trying to butter him up.

Yakimchuk flung off his arm, as if to knock Ribke's glass, and started to yell at him:

'This is a very grave state of affairs. We have to think with clear heads. It isn't some kind of children's charade. This is a matter of life and death. I've never met these people. How can you load them onto my hard-working shoulders as it's such a responsibility? Ribke, you have cooked up a horrendous situation and now you had better eat it. My conscience is clear. I'm not going to be trapped. I am off.'

The old man got ready to return home; however, it was now Mrs Yakimchuk's turn to speak. The old lady looked at us with such warmth and compassion; she smiled and crossed herself so many times that I ran out of numbers. Ten was then the extent of my counting proficiency – it didn't help that my schooling in the ghetto could best be described as somewhat limited. In fact, I had no formal education at all until I was six, by which age a child in other circumstances should certainly have been able to read, and to count far further than I could manage.

Mrs Yakimchuk fixed her crumpled skirt, took out the combs that held her hair up and rearranged it into a neat bun, then pulled her shoulders back. Looking so graceful, and with an assertive manner that proclaimed this was her usual way of addressing the old man when she had something important to announce, she spoke.

'Now listen, Yakimchuk . . .'

She never called him by his first name; I later wondered if he even had one.

She told her husband that if he refused to give us refuge, she would do it herself. And if she got caught, she would say he had nothing to do with it, it was all her idea. And then she warned him not to get angry again, because if he did, he could just take his horse and find somewhere else to live. Whatever the outcome was, all four of us – Mum, Haim, Shalom and I – would be coming home with her.

Mrs Yakimchuk was generally a very reserved and quiet lady, but when she had an opinion to express, she never minced her words. Her stubbornness knew no bounds. Mr Yakimchuk saw straight away that he had lost the battle. Although he never put up his hands in defeat, he did need a parting shot of sorts to satisfy his masculine pride. He told his wife angrily:

'You know what the trouble with your world is? Your God has the mind of a *baba* [old woman].'

She smiled knowingly; she could see he was defeated. He was well aware that 'God' was the only subject he could raise that would make her see red, and about which she would not compromise. She said:

'Well, you men didn't make this world an oasis of tranquillity.'

Mum then spoke up. She told Mr Yakimchuk that she could see perfectly clearly that he had good reason not to take us in. The risks were enormous. All she wanted to say was that she was just trying to do the best for three small, well-behaved children who had already lost their father and spent three years enduring hunger and the daily threat of death. And that he and Mrs Yakimchuk had the chance to save them from this hell.

And then she went to her battered leather satchel, pulled out a parcel containing all our remaining wealth and put it in Mr Yakimchuk's hand. At first he refused it, but Mum insisted, telling him that not only might he one day need it, but also that it would help her to retain her dignity as she threw her children on his and his wife's mercy. She never talked about herself: it was all about saving her children.

Mr Yakimchuk was stunned. He had a hard enough time with one strong-minded woman, but to be confronted by two in a united front – what chance did he stand?

Haim (Mum's financial advisor) then said: 'Why did you give him all you had in one go?' He spoke in Yiddish in the hope that Mr Yakimchuk would not understand. But the wise old owl got the gist: our city was – had been – very Jewish; Christians made up only about one third of the population.

Consequently, most of the non-Jews knew a bit of Yiddish through their daily dealings and this included Mr Yakimchuk.

Mum gave my brother a sideways glance, as if to say, 'Keep your counsel for another day.'

After all their wrangling, would Mr Yakimchuk take us or would he not? Beaten into grudging submission, he capitulated, and we were ushered onto his wagon where we lay down and he covered us with bales of straw. And then we were trundling along, the wooden boards hard on our skinny bodies. The journey must have been such a thrill for us children, an interlude where we left behind the barbed wire and daily fears of the ghetto for what we hoped would be safety. The cobbled city streets were soon behind us and then we were driving past fields and woods into the quiet of a country night.

Chapter 7

Uninvited Guests

It was just before dawn on a cold late November day when, disorientated and covered in straw, we arrived at the Yakimchuks' farm. It was about fifteen kilometres from the ghetto, but it could have been a universe away. This was an entirely new world for us. It was dark; the snow was drifting; and nobody in their right mind was out at such an ungodly hour, but still we hurried into the house, stepping into the kitchen, where the smell of baking bread and the warmth were overwhelming. After almost two years of confinement in the ghetto, it was beyond our wildest dreams. I could finally unbutton my own tattered coat; my hands were now so warm and nimble. The frost had vanished. It had evaporated into this new dawn, full of hope. Their home was sparsely furnished and there was no clutter. The Yakimchuks were pioneers of minimalism, half a century before it became chic.

We all sat in a circle on the floor in the back room to eat: Mr and Mrs Yakimchuk; their son, Ivan, his wife, Manka and their young children, Alexandra and Stefan, who looked at us as if we were aliens from another planet. Alexandra was about my age, Stefan a year or so younger. Mum spoke to them all in Ukrainian, but I didn't understand a word of that language, which was such a pity. Mrs Yakimchuk then produced a large basin containing what I came to know as her pièce de résistance, mashed potatoes, and the best, freshest newly baked bread ever. If there really was a heaven, at that moment, this was it.

And the grandchildren were right. We were as strange beings to them as they were to us. They were lovely kids, giggling away. It was so wonderful just to hear their laughter. Circumstances had led children like us to be sombre and silent.

I loved Mrs Yakimchuk's bread. During the months ahead, in my moments of generosity (which were rare), I would occasionally let the others have my portion of mash. But what I admired most were her painted wooden spoons. They were so beautifully decorated, with flowers and foliage and peasants dancing, all in the most vivid colours. I found these spoons intriguing, never having eaten off such beautiful objects. I licked them clean with passion just in case I left any trace of food.

For the next two days, Mum set about helping Mrs Yakimchuk with domestic chores. We never left the house in case someone saw us. All the doors were locked to stop uninvited guests wandering in, and at night, we climbed a ladder and got up into the rafters where there was hay for us to sleep on. Its aroma was intoxicating, somehow capturing sunshine, grass and sweet wildflowers. It was a fabulous space for us; such luxury. And it was where Mr Yakimchuk kept his apples and pears to ripen. They were well concealed, but my inquisitive brothers soon discovered their hiding place and could not resist scoffing one or two of them.

Mum warned us all: 'You mustn't eat the Yakimchuks' fruit. It is theirs for the winter. If they find out, they'll be very angry, and we will be out.'

But my brother Haim – whose role in our family increasingly resembled that of the Chancellor of the Exchequer in the British government – was more concerned about our own possessions, and asked Mum again why she hadn't kept some of them back, rather than giving them all to Mr Yakimchuk at once. Her response was most revealing:

'I fully understand your question. But you see, I have heard stories about Jewish people being taken in by Christians. They gave them part of their money, not all of it. So, what happened? The Christians only took them part of the way, and then murdered them and took the rest. I worked out that if I gave Mr and Mrs Yakimchuk the lot, with nothing left over, and we were fortunate enough to get to their place, I would know then that they were good people. At the end of the day, I didn't know if I could trust them. If they weren't genuine, they would have dropped us off along the way and had their stash. Why endanger themselves and bring us all the way home to here? So, once I entered their house, I knew we were in business.'

My brother nodded; now he understood.

When we first arrived, we spent most of the time in the rafters so as not to be seen by uninvited visitors, but we would come down at midday for food. On the second day, Mrs Yakimchuk wanted to show us that her cooking repertoire extended further than just mash, and she very proudly produced a soup, declaring triumphantly, 'Today you are having *bachlopke*.' It was hot and looked like a pool of water with potatoes floating in it. Then came chunks of bread, straight from the clay oven. How much better could life get?

On the third day of our lodgings with the Yakimchuks, while our feast was in full swing, there was a loud, insistent knocking at the front door. We dropped the beautiful spoons. Mum turned white, the blood draining from her face, and said she hoped nobody had seen us when we disembarked from the wagon.

Mrs Yakimchuk told her husband to answer the door and made a sign to Ivan to rush us out of the house and into the barn at the rear. We sat there fearfully, waiting to hear who the callers were. Mum whispered that it must have been relations visiting and that is why it took so long. Mr Yakimchuk finally appeared in a state of shock. He could barely tell us the grim news. He slowly took off his warm sheepskin coat, put it on the frozen earth floor and sat down. He gathered his strength and told us, to his sorrow, we must leave. We could hear it in his voice that he was sincerely sorry. He looked at us with a broken heart.

'This is not of my making. My life is completely shattered. It is beyond belief. The callers were a group of SS and Gestapo, along with a few Ukrainian collaborators. They came to set up a training centre here, in my house – *in my house* – using our outbuildings, including this barn and the cowshed.'

He explained that the place was going to be a centre for Ukrainians who were working with the SS and Gestapo against the Soviets. Mum was utterly stunned, desperately aware that our luck, until recently so good, looked as if it had now run out.

Mr Yakimchuk was in despair. He was a proud farmer, well established; the villagers had great respect for him. And now his house was going to be invaded by murderers and lowlifes.

Mrs Yakimchuk also saw the seriousness of the situation, but she would not be diverted from her normal routine: she came to the barn sighing and emitting heart-rending sighs of '*Bida, bida*' (Misfortune, misfortune), and then went off as usual to church. When she returned, she told her husband that she'd been to confession and told the priest about her current predicament.

'*What!*' screamed the old man, launching himself into the air with shocking vigour and rage. 'You told him that we are keeping Jews? He will be the first to tell the SS and the Gestapo.'

Not a good day for poor Mr Yakimchuk: first the SS and Gestapo at the door, now the involvement of the priest.

Mrs Yakimchuk stuck to her blazing guns, saying:

'My conscience is clear. I donated a gold chain to the church coffers so he can fix the leaking roof.'

This made my mum smile to herself: it was one of the items she had handed over to the Yakimchuks on arrival. It had belonged to her grandmother, who wore it to synagogue on high days and holidays to impress the women there, most of whom held their prayer books upside down because they were illiterate.

'*What!*' shouted the old man. 'You gave it to the priest! It will end up on his housekeeper's fat neck! I was going to give them everything back, as they won't be staying. They must leave.'

'They are going nowhere; they are staying here,' said Mrs

Yakimchuk, stamping her feet on the icy earth to emphasize her point.

'What do you mean "here"?'

'Right here,' she said emphatically. 'Ivan is on his way. You and he are going to dig out a pit. They will stay here. And, by the way, pick up your coat; you are ruining it. You might need it if you aren't preparing a place for them to stay. You might find yourself sleeping in the snow.'

The poor old man was just getting ready to unleash a barrage of curses at Mrs Yakimchuk when Ivan appeared, with a long face and a big shovel to dig out our new residence.

Mr Yakimchuk was extremely reluctant for us to continue to be his tenants in these altered circumstances, which threatened disaster for him, his family, the whole village – and most assuredly for us – if we were discovered. But in his household he was not the key decision-maker, he was merely a functionary.

Prompted by the thought that the entire German war machine appeared to be on its way to this particular farm, it didn't require a huge effort on our part to jump straight into this living grave. It was shallow and narrow, no more than 2.5 metres in length and breadth and 1.5 metres high. The earthen floor beneath it was covered in straw and, to keep us warm, we had a couple of blankets that Mum had managed to bring with us when we'd fled our previous lodgings in the ghetto. A large bucket was to be our toilet, which Mum put in a corner. If we turned our backs when it was in use, we could offer at least the illusion of privacy.

The top of the pit was covered in a thick pile of branches

and twigs, so that anybody who happened to enter the barn by chance would just see a pile of firewood. In their wildest dreams, they couldn't have imagined that several people were housed underneath. We sat on that frozen earthen floor, huddled together. It was a most harrowing time. We were in a constant almost total blackout, with just the slightest glimmer of light that penetrated through a hole in the barn roof and managed to work its way through the gaps between the twigs. Although it was all far from ideal, Mum said that, with the help of the Yakimchuks, there was a chance that we would survive the war. She also said she was sure that the Soviet army would defeat the Germans and that it wouldn't take too long. She was trying to give us hope. Mum seldom felt defeated, being so single-minded and confident that we would survive. It was reassuring for us kids.

She told us: 'We will come out of this hell. And you children will be free to spread your wings.'

Surely this did not include me, my brothers thought. I was too slow and too stubborn. At times I made their lives a misery. And I certainly didn't know when to keep quiet.

The first night in the pit passed rather quickly as we were so tired from all the squabbling with Mr Yakimchuk. But when we saw a fragment of light through the twigs we took it as a new beginning, hopefully the beginning of the end. Some flakes of snow had landed on the twigs through the gap in the roof. None of us had to get dressed because we were, as always, all ready to flee, fully dressed with our shoes on. At midday, Mrs Yakimchuk brought a black metal pot with very cold water for us to drink. It didn't take long for the contents of that to vanish.

Later she brought in a basin of mashed potatoes and freshly baked bread, but for some reason fell to her knees and crossed herself a few times. Not quite as many as when we were with Ribke: I could count all her prayers to the end, but she never stopped sighing. And her parting shot, as usual, was the mournful, '*Bida, bida.*' But for all her curious foibles, there was not enough gratitude in the world to bestow on that old lady, though I'm sure she knew just how grateful we were. Without her unshakeable support for us, Mr Yakimchuk would not have taken us in. She truly put her head on the block for us, poor Mrs Yakimchuk.

Chapter 8

The Pit

It was December 1943. We were becoming acclimatized to our frozen pit, although it took some further time to get used to its sunless nature. And the barn that hosted our new abode was itself neither in its first flush of youth nor the best of health. It had to struggle with every sinew of its fabric against the ferocious, howling Siberian gales that beat mercilessly against its elderly timber walls; and its sagging roof was buckling under the suffocating weight of snow. And yet it somehow managed to remain heroically upright, providing a priceless sanctuary for one lone, determined woman and her three children, so desperate to evade the evil of the times.

In order that we could distinguish day from night, Ivan had deliberately left unmended a small opening in the roof of the barn; and we were so very grateful for any sliver of light that penetrated into our dark and inhospitable grave. But such a benefit did not come without its price. And the 'price' was that the twigs shielding our pit were regularly covered with snow that had frozen solid. Whenever the Yakimchuks came to see us, they had first to break through the frozen snow there; and, quite often, the protecting twigs snapped and a new consignment had to be gathered. We felt extremely guilty to have heaped so much more difficulty upon these old folks, as if they didn't have enough to deal with already. What a poisoned chalice we were proving to be.

It was hard to keep track of the passing days but when she thought it was around the time of Hanukkah, Mum told us about the Jewish festival of light and the beautiful spiral candles in vivid colours that would be lit in the silver menorah that her sister, Fruma, had brought from Russia as a wedding present for my parents. (Fruma lived in Russia for a while but couldn't find kosher food, so eventually returned to Ludmir and was killed at Piatydni.) Mum loved Hanukkah. It was such a joyous time, when we didn't commemorate defeat or enslavement. It was a time when Judah drove the Syrians out of Jerusalem and the holy temple, which they had defiled, was cleansed. The golden menorah was lit again, and for eight days they celebrated.

How I wished that we could have a Hanukkah like the one Mum was describing. Maybe next year, I thought hopefully.

In the evening, Mrs Yakimchuk came with a fresh loaf of bread and a pot of ice-cold water straight from the well. As she was shooing away the snow from the twigs with her bare hands, we felt so helpless at not being able to help the old lady. If only we could have cleared the snow from her path and broken up the ice to stop her from slipping. It was just before Christmas when she found us all huddling together, consumed with fear and cold; and she knelt to pray for better days.

(Actually, Mrs Yakimchuk was constantly praying. How she didn't get frostbitten knees, I have no idea.) She told us that she wasn't going to make a fuss about Christmas. For her, Easter was the time she went to town, and so she was going to give Christmas a miss. I was always glad when she could stay a little longer to talk to Mum and give us all hope.

Mum asked Mrs Yakimchuk if it would be possible for her to bring us a few drops of oil so that she could make a wick from a tattered blanket, insert the handle of a metal spoon into the earthen wall, then fill the bowl of the spoon with oil, dip the wick in and light a flame to warm hands that could barely function in the debilitating cold. Mrs Yakimchuk nodded in agreement; she promised to try her best, then left in the traditional way, intoning, '*Bida, bida.*'

Once the long night had given way to the short day, the old lady returned, wrapped in a huge blanket and holding a few matches and a small rusty tin embellished with German script. The top of the tin had got lost and been replaced with a bit of old twisted linen to prevent the snow from getting in and contaminating the fuel inside, since that could stop it from igniting.

Mum had an amazing practical ability to create good from very little. I suspect it came from having been brought up on a farm where people had to be inventive and resourceful; she possessed the most extraordinary amount of pure common sense. And, thanks to Mrs Yakimchuk's generosity, Mum was able to light a flame in our shadow-world and lift our spirits. Hanukkah had come to Biscobich, and we all basked in its light and relished the hope it gave us.

The following day, we heard the sound of someone trying to open the barn door. There were none of Mr Yakimchuk's normal 'endearments', as he cursed the elements. And he was always very nimble with the door in any case, even when the wind outside was playing havoc. This time, it was the sound of someone unfamiliar with the barn. And we could hear heavy footsteps crushing the frozen earthen floor; strong, plodding footsteps, not like Yakimchuk's deliberate, heavy strides. Our stomachs were heavy with dread. Had someone noticed the flame?

Suddenly, we heard a voice call out Mum's name. She gave a huge sigh of relief and exclaimed, 'It's Ribke!' As Christmas was just around the corner, he had come to visit his family. When he saw us all huddled together around our little flame, he couldn't prevent a tear from falling and blemishing his grey quilted coat, fastened with a black leather belt, to stop the arctic gales from ripping it off.

'Ribke, what a surprise! We never thought we'd see you so soon. Have you seen your uncle?'

'Not yet. I thought I'd leave that pleasure for last.'

Mum smiled. As he commiserated with us and our situation, he couldn't stop shaking his head in despair.

Mum asked how it was back in Ludmir's ghetto. Had he seen Rachel? Ribke was pleased to say that she had left the city and headed west. Then she asked about Uncle Hirsch. As his mood instantly turned sombre, Mum guessed the news was not good. Hirsch had been shot while trying to swim across the river to escape. Mum looked straight at Haim. As bad as it was here, at least her eldest son hadn't gone with Uncle Hirsch to meet the same fate.

Ribke then told us that the ghetto had been completely obliterated and that all the people there were either taken away by the SS to the forest near the village of Chvalnitz (also called Falemicze) where they were machine-gunned and their bodies burned. There were rumours people had been burned alive. No one survived. That included the head of the Jewish Council, Kudish, who was rounded up like the rest, along with his wife and son. (I later found out that there was also a group of 120 Jews who had united in hopes of joining the partisans to fight the Germans alongside the Poles; but instead, the Poles had rounded them up and shot the lot in a place called Vorotshin.)

Ribke had felt sickened bringing us such dire news. Just coming here was hard, with the city littered with the bodies of the dead. He described it as being like one vast field of snow with corpses waiting for God.

'Did nobody run away?'

'No', he said. 'And those already in the countryside and in the forest who had been hiding with Gentiles actually came back to the ghetto.'

'What fools! Why, Ribke?'

'The German military command issued an order for all people to register. Then, they would be given new official documents and there would be no more exterminations.'

Mum shook her head. 'The mere mention of "exterminations" should have alerted them,' she said.

'Well, people could not bring themselves to believe that this was all just a ploy to round up all the others who were still alive in order to kill them all in one go.'

'Such gullibility,' said Mum, trying to restrain her anger. 'And we are meant to be the clever ones.'

Ribke shook his head in despair, apologizing for the bleak news he brought. Giving Mum a sad smile, he told her to 'keep the flame burning'. He brushed the last few traces of icicles and snow away from the steadfast twigs that were witness to our ordeal; and then, shaking his head in disbelief, he left.

In late December 1943, Mr Yakimchuk, who had also unwittingly taken on the role of our war correspondent, ran into the barn, bursting with exhilaration. He was absolutely covered in soot from cleaning the oven, but he just couldn't wait to heave aside the pile of branches and twigs that were shielding us from discovery. He announced that Kiev had been liberated, and proceeded to praise Nikolai Vatutin, the Red Army general who had taken the city on 6 November but then been in a fight to hold it in the face of German attacks. Now it seemed that the Germans had been pushed back. 'I knew it. I *knew* it!', he kept saying, punching the air with his blackened fist. He was full of joy. 'I knew Vatutin would do it.' It sounded as if the Soviet commander had won the whole war single-handed. We, of course, were overjoyed to see Mr Yakimchuk in such a triumphant mood. Perhaps, just perhaps, there actually might be real cause for hope at last.

The battle for Kiev had been bloody; hundreds of thousands of soldiers and civilians were killed or wounded over the course of the war, though it was impossible to quantify how many had suffered injury or death in battle rather than simply succumbed to the pitiless cold. Battalions of captured Wehrmacht soldiers would never see their Fatherland again. Although the Red Army had managed to secure Kiev, the third largest city of the Soviet Union, the sacrifice for this achievement went far beyond anything anyone could have imagined. It would be a gross understatement to simply call Kiev's liberation a bittersweet victory. Few other cities endured as much in the Second World War. Two years before this liberation, the Nazis had tried to wipe Kiev off the face of the Earth.

On Christmas Day, Mrs Yakimchuk came out in a very sombre mood, telling us that Paraska, her daughter, had taken a turn for the worse, and she didn't think she could last much longer. And the cold weather was not helping; nor the unending, self-inflicted human tragedy wrought by humankind in the form of war that insistently imposed itself upon us all.

Mum commiserated with the old woman. If only times had been different, she would have been in a position to offer help that could have ensured Paraska had a chance to recover and live a full young life. Mum felt so much for Mrs Yakimchuk, a lady with so much goodness and holiness who was watching her child fade away in such pain.

We always looked forward to Mrs Yakimchuk's visits to our hideout. She was our ray of golden sunshine. When she came, she would bring water and, of course, her mash. Sometimes she mixed it with swine fat. It was such an improvement, even though somehow the lumps that accompanied her dish insisted on lodging themselves in my throat. But no one in the whole world could make bread as good as Mrs Yakimchuk's.

That is how we passed the day, or maybe it was the night. It was hard to tell, since so little light could penetrate the opening in the roof. At this time, the late December skies were laden with heavy clouds of snow. The cold completely permeated our bodies. It was lucky Mum had had the foresight to bring some blankets. I don't think the Yakimchuks had any to spare. They had their ailing daughter, their son and his wife and their grandchildren to keep warm.

We all tried desperately not to ask for any creature comforts so as not to put any more pressure on them or give Mr Yakimchuk any further reason to tell us to go. We just took what we were given and we could not have been more grateful.

We children were quite well behaved, considering all the hardships we were enduring. Mum kept us in check by quietly telling us stories about our past, about our father and grandparents, about the village where we used to visit the farmhouse and play hide and seek in the orchard. My brothers were very quick to interrupt Mum by saying that I was rubbish and not good at hiding. It's such a pity we can't play that game now, since I've subsequently become rather good at it.

As we were listening to one of Mum's stories, Mr Yakimchuk appeared, looking solemn. We could tell immediately that he was not bearing good news. He said the Germans and their collaborators were settling in the house and were going to gather their new recruits to work in conjunction with them.

My mum's heart sank as we had all just witnessed the old man actually running out of ideas right before our eyes. 'Well, we must wait until the morning to see what they are bringing with them.'

The barn was adjacent to a large cowshed. By now, the Yakimchuks had got rid of their cow, which had been ready for the abattoir in any case. The present occupant was Mr Yakim-chuk's beloved horse, to which he would pour out his abundant emotions. That animal was his salvation, the one that listened compassionately to all his sorrows. He passed his finest moments with that horse, who never gave him an ounce of grief.

The barn and the cowshed were partitioned by a makeshift wall built from planks of wood that barely fitted each other. Between the planks were sizeable gaps that it was possible to see through without much effort. The gaps needed to be plugged somehow, but before we could do anything about them, just two days later, we heard the almightiest commotion outside our pit.

From our well-hidden location, we heard loud voices in German coming from very close by, seemingly engaged in a robust argument. We gathered immediately that the German troops were already here with their horses, which were also making quite a racket. Outside, nearby, we could hear clanking chains and heavy rolling machinery; clearly they had brought heavy fighting equipment with them.

Our hearts stopped as we waited to hear how Mr Yakim-chuk would react to this invasion. This time, we felt the writing was on the wall, and what we read there was not remotely palatable.

The Germans still appeared to be standing by the door, organizing the housing of their huge Belgian horses and all their equipment. Mr Yakimchuk stood talking to them in his limited German, which he had last used in the Great War. He was explaining that this barn was not suitable for the needs of such important guests. Its roof was full of holes, and it was clearly not suitable for the heavy machinery. And their fabulous horses deserved far better lodgings. He was going to remove his own horse from the cowshed and bring it into the barn with us, so that the cowshed was now entirely free for the Germans' use alone. He spun them a yarn that, in the village, they had a custom that they always gave the best to newcomers; because they were the guests, they should be treated with the utmost courtesy.

When Mr Yakimchuk first ushered his closest confidant into the barn, it was almost like a funeral procession. He held him so dear to his heart; his steps were slow and his body stooped, as if in mourning. Peering through the twigs that framed our pit, we could see that he actually took off his hat out of respect for that unruly animal. He had him on a rope that was going to be anchored next to the entrance to the barn. But when the old man had first tried, with great trepidation, to tie him up, his old horse suddenly found a new lease of life, kicking his hooves like a young colt. His lameness seemed to vanish in a flash. I wondered if it was all just an act, put on whenever he didn't want to gallop in the cold or struggle in the fields with Mr Yakimchuk's heavy plough.

The old man was careful as he tethered the horse, hoping he hadn't been too harsh as he tied a flimsy knot. And there was a bag of carrots for him, as well as further compassionate words of comradeship.

As the horse was being introduced to his new residence, we could hear in the distance '*Bida, bida.*' Mrs Yakimchuk was on her way. After a quick glance at her husband's handiwork, she said: 'Yakimchuk, this rope is not going to do the job. It's too weak, and there are too many knots. This won't last a day.'

When Mr Yakimchuk heard these comments, he was furious and lashed out at her:

'Now, Baba, you come here just to criticize my work. Work I wouldn't have to do at all if not for your godly deeds. This is all your fault. If you hadn't agreed to bring this lot here in the first place, I would not have to do this in here and my horse could have stayed in the cowshed. And the German bastards, killers, murderers or whatever you wish to call them, they could have had this barn instead for all their bloody horses and clobber.'

Although Mrs Yakimchuk sympathized with what her husband was saying and all the hardships he was enduring, she pointed out that he was blaming the wrong person. She told him that it wasn't her fault, or his fault, or the fault of the three children and their mother who they were sheltering, it was the fault of a gangster in Berlin. She then told him in no uncertain terms to stop feeling sorry for himself and his spoiled horse and to spare a thought for the four people having to live in silence in a dark and frozen world.

She didn't want to hurt him too deeply; after all, he was doing the best he could under such tough circumstances. He was labouring away, all on his own, without his son to help him. Then Mrs Yakimchuk took a huge, thick rope out of her basket, handed it to him and said: 'This will do the job, Yakimchuk.'

The old man looked at her, fuming with rage. 'If you are so clever, why are you always so late? You should have spent less time with your priest.' He always threw in the priest when he felt beaten by her. 'Now listen to me, the horse is tied up, I'm certainly not going to undo my hard work. It stays just as it is.' He rubbed his hands together; he wasn't going to budge.

In our pit, we were utterly despondent, with our presence here adding to the cares of this old couple. Mum in particular felt so dejected. She had always been a very independent, self-reliant woman and now, here we were, creating such hardship for the Yakimchuks. If only their son Ivan had been home to give them a hand. But unfortunately, he had been conscripted by the SS, along with other Ukrainians, to work alongside them. How ridiculously ironic: the Yakimchuks' son with the SS while his family harboured a Jewish mother and three small children. Where was the rationale there? Where was the sanity? What kind of world were we living in?

Although we were aware that Mr Yakimchuk now had extremely limited access to the barn at night, and even though our ears had become well attuned to all the sounds around us, he was so quiet that we could only just make out his approaching footsteps. He shook with fear as he told us about this new situation and admitted that he could not see a way out of the danger. Somehow, we must try to live with it; hopefully, the Germans would not be inquisitive enough to venture into the barn. His main concern seemed to be for his horse: how was the animal going to adapt to the new setting, especially being tied up with a rope?

'He is such a free spirit,' said the old man mournfully.

A Mother's Courage

We truly felt for Mr Yakimchuk. Like us, he was a victim of a cruel world, and in his heart of hearts he was really soft-natured. A good, kind man. Just before he left, he took a loaf of bread from his pocket. As in many moments of despair, we had a glimpse of joy. And in the old man's inner pocket were a few baked potatoes. He didn't dare risk being seen carrying a basin with mash, in case he encountered some of his new, uninvited guests. His hands were blackened from the potatoes, which had been baked over coal. I loved those potatoes: they were so, so sumptuous.

Before the old man left he stopped to have a word with his poor old horse. Yesterday, he was king of the cowshed; today, he had become Prisoner Number Five. And he wasn't even Jewish. Mr Yakimchuk reassured him that better days would come, and that he would again one day be free, no more rope or rickety barn. He patted the horse on his back and wished him goodnight.

That wretched horse. What had he done wrong that he was now forced to share his home with us? On the positive side, though, before this move to his new accommodation, the animal had always had to wait for Mr Yakimchuk's visits to cheer him up and relieve some of the tedium. Now, in his new environment, it had four people constantly available to listen to any imaginary problems he might wish to share.

Chapter 9

Under Siege

The snow and ice never left; nor did the Germans, forever coming and going with their horses and their shouting and swear words and their tales of great achievements – cleansing the world of flea-infested Jews. They had put makeshift toilets, with walls of plaited straw, up against the wall of the barn, uncomfortably close to our pit. They liked to brag to each other when using the facilities, so we could hear all their fine adventures from the night before. All their boasting was making Mum angry, so I wished they would keep their stories to themselves. At times, the whole yard was littered with masses of their hardware; sometimes, for many days on end, we had to go without any food whatsoever. During such times of want, I even longed for Mrs Yakimchuk's lumpy mash.

After Soviet victories began to turn things round in 1943, the Germans found themselves on the back foot. They had lost many thousands of soldiers, many taken as prisoners to work in the Russian Gulags. Their kit no longer matched up to the standard of the Soviets', their tanks were sitting ducks as they ran out of petrol, and their own supplies were unable to reach them because of the harsh weather, the vastness of the country and the lack of infrastructure. To add to their problems, Göring's Luftwaffe was stretched to the limit. The Germans didn't have as many planes as the Soviets and the ones they had were defending the Fatherland. The factories in Russia were working at full capacity, churning out vast supplies of weapons and planes, a non-stop production line they had the slave labour to man. But, most of all, Soviet military personnel were accustomed to the harsh winters of their country, the most lethal weapon at their disposal. They also had General Georgy Zhukov, who wasn't shy of pushing as many soldiers as were needed right up to the front line. The German army was thinly spread across an enormous Eastern Front, feeling demoralized and defeated. To counter this, a new gang of Ukraine fighters had been dreamed up by Heinrich Himmler and the butcher Otto Wächter, who had overseen the extermination of Jews in Krakow and western Ukraine. The SS Galizien Division had been recruiting since June 1943, with support from a number of Ukrainian nationalist parties and organizations, including more moderate politicians. It had been agreed that the Galizien Division would only fight the Russians, not any of the Western Allies.

We were all now solely in the hands of the gods, those same gods who blew so hot and cold on our fortunes.

As we sat in our pit, hail pounded down from the skies, and chunks of ice hung suspended from the barn's roof. The wind

outside howled at gale-force and it felt as if the whole makeshift structure was being torn apart, assisted by the ferocious
elements.

'The world has lost its will to live,' Mum muttered.

We were under siege. The Germans were all over Mr Yakimchuk's land. We could hear them from the cowshed next
door – banging away, loading their ammunition onto the
wagons, bragging that last night they were so lucky, coming
across a group of 'little Jewish bastards' wandering about.

'We rounded them up. You should have heard them screaming for their mothers, the Jewish whores.'

'Tonight is going to be a good night. The old man's moon-
shine is going to flow.'

Poor Mum was listening to this and understanding it. My
brothers caught the odd word, like *Judisch*. Over the past few
years they had become familiar with insults flung at them by
the German invaders.

'These thick-headed creatures – they can't even speak properly; their German is so poor. They are ignorant savages,' Mum
said later, when they had gone and the farmyard was quiet once
more. 'Mr Yakimchuk will take good care of us. He is a brave
soldier. He fought in the Great War.'

Needless to say, quite soon we children were swearing in
German like old troopers. Mr Yakimchuk knew a bit of that
language, and when he came to see us we three would show off
our latest naughty words and he would howl with laughter,
which always put him in an excellent mood. Mum told him
about the hullaballoo the previous day. He said he knew that
the bastards drank all his *samagon*, his homemade vodka. He

kept hiding the bottles, but they always managed to get hold of them.

'I'm forever scratching my head, trying to think where I should put my precious brew. You see, last year we had a good harvest, a large crop of potatoes. My son is a good brewer but he could not get enough bottles, so we had to put some in barrels. This year, with this snow and cold weather, we had a bad year, and we couldn't brew so much. This is now the least of my worries. You lot come at the very top in terms of causing me sleepless nights. The Germans have taken Ivan away to dig trenches for Hitler's army. I hope he's safe. His mother prays all day. And now you would not believe it but the priest has become a regular visitor, reassuring my wife that her son is safe, that God will watch over him. I have a feeling the real reason he's coming is to have a taste of my brew. And my wife thinks he is saintly! Good luck to both of them.

'But for heaven's sake, you must not tell my wife what I said about the priest. I let her go with him, to get on with him if it gives her comfort. So now I have the SS, the Gestapo and even the priest helping themselves to my *samagon*. The only good thing about you lot is that you don't drink.'

Mr Yakimchuk was in fact a god-fearing man who went to church, so I don't think he really begrudged the priest having a sip of his brew. He did resent the influence the man had over Mrs Yakimchuk, though.

Mum used to like Mr Yakimchuk's visits when he was in a good mood. But when he was in a bad mood, worried about the danger we posed to his family, he would bring us a crumpled piece of paper on which he'd drawn a map showing the way back to Ludmir and tell us it was time for us to go. The arrival of Mrs Yakimchuk and her '*Bida, bida*' would prompt him to snatch the map back, as he knew exactly what his saintly wife would say. This time, in an effort to prevent another such threat, Mum suggested that he might like to store his fine brew in our château:

'You know we would not touch it. It will be secure as long as we are here.'

The old man burst out laughing. 'What, next to that smelly bucket full of shit? That we must empty and try not to be seen with?'

Mum nodded. 'Yes. We live with it but we do not notice it any longer. Mind you, Yakimchuk, in comparison to your horse's habits, it smells sweet. Why don't you get rid of the lame good-for-nothing? It is more work for you.'

Mr Yakimchuk looked at Mum in astonishment.

'You say that? If I take out this poor lame creature, that would mean the end of us all – you, my family, the villagers and even the priest. That horse is our salvation. When I come out of here, carrying that bucket of yours, and someone sees me, they say "Phew! What is that smell, Mr Yakimchuk?" I say, "You know, it's my poor horse." People don't hang around and ask too many questions about where it is from after that. They run a mile. The smell is too strong for them. If I let my horse go, that'll be the end of us. The whole bloody German cavalry will be here with their horses.'

The old man struggled to stand up – the cold earth did not help – and gave a big sigh: 'Oh children, children.' He brushed off the cold damp soil from his long-ribbed coat and put a finger to his lips. 'Shush, not a word to my wife about that priest. The most important thing is that we have to keep him sweet. He is the only one in the village who knows you are here. In a way, we are in his "godly" hands. As long as he puts in a good word for Ivan, he can have as much of my *samagon* as he likes.'

Chapter 10

Make-Believe

Mum could not stand up in that pit. It was too low for her. She could only kneel. For us kids, it wasn't that bad, as we were quite small. At night we three would sleep while Mum kept watch in case we made noises; if we did, she could give us a nudge to be quiet. During the day, Mum would have a nap. She was a very light sleeper: at the slightest noise she would wake up to check we didn't have uninvited guests. The truth is we hardly slept. We were famished, badly short of water and shivering from the bitter cold; our blankets were shredded and, worst of all, we lived with the constant fear of being discovered by our raucous, murderous neighbours.

They were not very kind or polite about us. I couldn't understand why they didn't like us. We never disturbed their 'peaceful' goings-on. We never threw a ball into their gardens. One day we heard them yelling '*Heraus! Heraus!*' and, conditioned by our time in the ghetto, we hurried to obey. As we three started to climb out of our pit, Mum grabbed hold of us.

'They're not shouting for us to come out, they're shouting for the horses,' she whispered.

Mum struggled to get the boys to stay in. I was more of a follower; I was the one who was dragged along. Dealing with two young boys could sometimes be a pain for Mum, although looking back I wonder if I was any less of a problem: after all, they were seven and five years older than me and could be reasoned with; I was only four and there was always the concern that I might get upset and make a noise that would betray us.

I was also the dumb one with no imagination, but I got on well with Haim, who was quite high-spirited and lively. Mr Yakimchuk liked him a lot, too; Haim made him chuckle. Haim was the quintessential escapee. His escapes were so real, he would struggle into his old and too-small coat and he would set off (in his imagination). He could remember to the last detail all the places where he had hidden or skied or skated before we were locked down in the ghetto. He would describe his hiding place so vividly that it sounded completely real to me. He would demonstrate just how he skied and how he skated. I was always ready to join him, but in reality we never went anywhere; we had to stay hidden where we were, and try to stay away from danger as best we could.

My middle brother Shalom was very passive. He lived in cloud-cuckoo-land and was rather selfish. When our daily ration arrived, which consisted of a small basin of mashed potatoes and some bread, Mum divided the mash into four portions. Shalom would insist on eating last, just in case there was a crumb more left in the basin. This irritated me no end, as did his imaginary friend whom he called 'Schpitalner Mensch', a term that meant nothing to anyone but him. He was enthralled by this dreamed-up creature, who would bring him books, paper to write on and accompany him to school. What kind of twit was he? Most boys of his age would have dreamed of skating, climbing and playing football. Poor Mum was beside herself when he kept banging on about his 'friend'. Although she began to think that her son might be losing his mind, in a strange way, it might have been that imagination which kept him sane. He was creating a land of make-believe, full of hope for sure.

My imagination went no further than wondering when Mrs Yakimchuk was coming with baked potatoes. I thought that being in a pit was normal, and that was just how people every-where lived. I had only been three years old when we had gone into the ghetto, where we didn't exactly live the high life, so generally I just accepted our situation. I never had a bath, my shoes were full of holes, and the rag that I had been wearing for two years was falling apart. My skin was bright red from scratching flea bites. My best time was when Mrs Yakimchuk came. I adored that lady and I think she had a bit of a soft spot for me, or it might just have been that she pitied me, I'm not sure. I wasn't a very fussy eater, but then again, there wasn't much to be fussy about. But – there's always a 'but' – as I've mentioned before, I did not like Mrs Yakimchuk's mash. It was so lumpy I just couldn't swallow it. My main dish of the day was bread, which I still love to this day. Mum would give me her portion and hide another small bit for me, so I could have it in the morning for breakfast. That was the time when I was most hungry, as I had skipped Mrs Yakimchuk's lumpy fodder the day before.

I felt very bad not doing full justice to her carefully prepared mash. I never actually admitted it to her, though, and I kept it a secret for the greater part of my life, as she was the last person I would ever wish to insult. She made the best baked potatoes in the whole wide world and beyond. They were perfumed with holiness – when she was delivering them, she hid them in her armpits and, because washing facilities at the Yakimchuks' place were non-existent, so the potatoes were scented with her own very personal sweetness.

Sometimes, when the morning came, I would look for my bread and find that, alas, it had disappeared. I would weep for my breakfast. Mum would put her hand on my mouth so as not to waken our neighbours, but I couldn't stop my tears from flowing. I was very cross and often interrogated my fellow pit-mates. 'Where is it?' I noticed my brothers looking sheepish, but surely they would not dare lay their hands on my bread? Mum would convincingly defend her sons, and she certainly would not eat my breakfast herself. In order to put a stop to my complaints, she would conclude that our friends, the mice, had come during the night and eaten my bread.

One Sunday Mrs Yakimchuk came straight from church with a loaf of fresh bread tucked under her big shawl. In view of the current situation, Mrs Yakimchuk told Mum that delivering food safely and unnoticed was becoming too dangerous and that a new plan had to be found.

But before such a plan could even begin to be considered, Mum's attention was drawn in admiration to Mrs Yakimchuk's brand-new felt boots. The old lady gave an innocent, shy giggle. 'Oh, my boots for Sunday best. When Ribke came for Christmas, he managed somehow to get me a new pair. They're a bit too big, which, in a way, is a blessing, so I can wrap my feet with some old rags to keep warm. My old leather boots were falling apart. They'd been patched up so often, you could hardly see the old leather. And the soles were falling to pieces as well. Leather is not at its best in the snow, which rots it away in no time.'

'I'm so pleased to see you in your new felt boots. I hope they keep you lovely and warm,' said Mum.

Mrs Yakimchuk went on: 'The ladies in the church were looking enviously at my boots. I felt so embarrassed. I wish they could all have boots like mine. Ribke is such a wonderful nephew. I wish that my Yakimchuk would be more benevolent towards him, if only to say thank you for the sausages he managed to barter for a bottle of vodka.'

We all found this talk of everyday life so wonderful; it was a reminder that there was still a world – in which some sort of normality was possible – going on outside the narrow confines of our pit.

Mum suggested to Mrs Yakimchuk it might be possible to dig a small service tunnel between our earthen walls and the farmyard outside, through which food could be pushed in to us. Between meals, the opening could be stuffed with hay. If the Yakimchuks' dog was then brought out and fed close to the outer entrance of the tunnel, it would look as if the arrangement was for him and him alone, and no one would give it any further thought.

When the old lady went back to the house, she proudly told her husband about the ingenious new plan that she and my mother had devised for a tunnel. Mr Yakimchuk characteristically hit the ceiling.

'What next!' he cried.

Well, 'next' turned out to be Ivan, who came with an axe and a shovel. For a brief, fleeting moment during his excavations, we looked out through the cavity. Yes, there was still life out there.

Now – like true prisoners of war – we were the proud possessors of a tunnel, and provisions could once again be passed more freely through to our hiding place. However, as happens in many great projects, an unanticipated spanner appeared in the works. Whenever the dog was looking for some amusement, he would stick his head into the tunnel, and in doing so push the hay plug into our pit. So we had to push the hay back into the mouth of the tunnel in order to disguise the opening again. Back and forth this went. In assessing the ultimate victor in this fine game, I must say, the dog won paws down.

Having four human beings confined within such a small, damp, squalid, lightless place was never going to be anything other than extraordinarily harsh. Mum would try to fill the days with stories, and food was an occasional distraction, but generally we spent our time staring at the shadowy earthen walls, trying to kill the lice that infested us and dreaming that Mr Yakimchuk would come with some baked potatoes (and no map) and tell us what a brave soldier he was.

Poor Mr Yakimchuk. We could invariably hear him sighing heavily, releasing his huge puffs of air as he made his way into the barn. Whenever his mind filled with doubt and worry, he would lash out and vent his anger on us, or else blame his wayward nephew for his misfortune, always insinuating that it would be better if we left. Mum could well understand his point of view. She could see all the many difficulties that weighed so heavily upon the old farmer's shoulders: his daughter was seriously ill; his beloved horse had had to be unceremoniously rehoused to give space to the bloody Gestapo; his son had been conscripted to undertake work for the SS; his home had – unbelievably – become a centre for young Ukrainian lads to be fast-tracked into the German army; and the cowshed apparently had become host to half the German cavalry. And as if all this was not enough, the cherry on this calamitous cake was the four of us. Mum would listen to his distress attentively and nod her head in sympathy. She understood him so well. They were both, in their different ways, caught up in a dark catastrophe that was not of their own making.

I remember once Mr Yakimchuk had just about finished unburdening himself of his heavy consignment of woes and was ready to go when he suddenly said, 'Ah, I forgot that I had some potatoes in my pocket. Mrs Yakimchuk is going to kill me for staying so long. The chimney is blowing soot; it's about time it was cleaned.'

Mr Yakimchuk left, muttering disconsolately to himself. I'm absolutely certain that his life would have been so much easier if we had actually left; but he knew that Mrs Yakimchuk would never let that happen. And he found himself well and truly caught on the horns of this ever-present dilemma.

But equally, in his heart of hearts, he also knew that he would never willingly drive us out to become prey to the insatiable savages outside, who would always be eager to spill our blood. He was far too proud a man and much too brave a soldier.

Chapter 11

Calamity

It was January 1944, and the flimsy knots on the horse's rope were still intact, if only just. Mrs Yakimchuk kept a close eye on that horse and the fragile rope. She did not have much faith in either the animal or her husband's ability to control it. We waited with interest to see if the old man would come down from his high horse (excuse the pun) and swap the rope over to the more suitable one that his wise wife had offered him. But he was too proud to give in to 'Baba', and we, in the pit, had no say in the matter. But even if we had, we definitely wouldn't have offered any advice, and nor would it have been taken. We, after all, were just miserable, troublesome squatters, posing a daily danger to the family.

The ferocity of the winter snows was still raging, and the Red Army was gaining ground, but nothing like fast enough for us. Mum fretted: 'Even if they were walking on stilts, they should have been here by now.' The Germans were busily reinforcing their troops with the newly formed Corps of Ukrainians, added to help them halt the Soviet advance.

One of the upsides of this was that our neighbours from next door had gone away to fight against the Soviets. But there were still enough Ukrainian collaborators on the lookout for Jews to fill their wells that we had to remain careful not to attract their attention.

Mum's moods now were getting quite dark, as she had to deal with the three of us – all so very different – while struggling to maintain the status quo. My middle brother Shalom was the one who gave Mum the most concern. He was the least vocal, which was a worry in itself, and he became very inward-looking. He only ever looked forward to one thing: his portion of mash, which had to be left till last. This quirk was starting to annoy Haim, usually the most tolerant of us all. And worse still, Shalom had begun to dream again about Schpitalner Mensch, his invented hero, though in fact he, in such a strange way, proved ultimately to be his mental salvation.

As we were squatting in our dwelling, consumed with boredom, suddenly and without any warning the old horse somehow managed to free himself. Having snapped his rope, the horse, as surprised as the rest of us at his sudden freedom, lurched into the pit, completely demolishing our home and burying us alive into the bargain. With him came mounds of earth and the contents of the shit bucket, all intermingled on top of us. The four of us tried desperately to push the horse back out, but his weight was quite beyond our strength. He was stuck fast amongst us, flailing desperately in his attempts to escape the pit, and making the most peculiar noises.

Unfortunately, the only person who spoke his language was late delivering his water and carrots. And us? We were being suffocated by the great beast. If help didn't arrive quickly, we all felt it might prove the end of our odyssey.

After what felt like hours but may just have been minutes, we finally heard Mr Yakimchuk approaching, breathing heavily as he struggled with the weight of the horse's supplies. When he came into the barn, he let out a scream, 'Where is my horse?' For a few seconds he couldn't see the animal anywhere, as he was obscured in the pit amongst all the debris and us, furiously doing his best to get away from these squatters who for so long had been encroaching upon his space.

Mr Yakimchuk rushed up, and within minutes he was joined in the rescue attempt by Mrs Yakimchuk, Manka and – such luck! – Ivan, who had been given a few days off from his digging. (Poor fellow, home for a rest and here there was yet more of the same kind of work.) Mrs Yakimchuk ran to her basket, fetched the thick rope and threw it to Ivan, who used it to tether his father's animal to his own, which then pulled the stranded creature out of the pit. The Yakimchuks then set about rescuing the crushed pit-dwellers.

We looked at our home with sad affection – it wasn't what anybody in normal circumstances would have chosen, but it was all we had, and we were immensely grateful for it. Yet now it lay in ruins.

Mum was shattered. Every inch of our bodies was covered in a horrible mixture of mud, smashed twigs and the contents of the waste bucket. She looked at us and kept her tears back, trying desperately not to make a dreadful situation even worse. We children also kept our composure, trying hard to suppress our own emotions.

Then Mrs Yakimchuk started to lay into her husband: 'This was all your fault, not changing that useless rope.'

Ivan, the gentlest of souls, suggested she save the insults for a later date, since it would be more productive to keep a level head and come to some sort of solution to bring this situation under control and work out the next step, if indeed there was one.

We four sat on the icy barn floor, completely deflated. Our limbs were aching from the unequal fight, and we also had some cuts and grazes, which we were trying to conceal so as not to make the old man feel even more guilty. What concerned us most was the thought that the old farmer would now have had more than enough of us and would finally insist that we should leave.

Mum had a quiet word with Ivan. Perhaps the time to leave was now right, she mused, as there were fewer Germans about. Maybe it really was time to go. Ivan, however, absolutely dismissed Mum's idea. He was adamant that there were still a substantial number of collaborators about. Worse, he told her, they were more active than ever, now that their powers were waning. And such people would not think twice about murdering anyone they regarded as their enemy. He spoke passionately, telling Mum how ashamed he was of those of his countrymen who'd collaborated with the invaders, and he insisted that she and her children should not even think about moving out. He himself would rebuild the pit, and in the meantime Mum and we three children must come into the house for a couple of days.

Ivan himself was, of course, also effectively a collaborator, but only because he had no alternative. He was a Ukrainian nationalist, not a Nazi sympathizer, and above all had nothing whatever in common with the SS.

And then he spoke to Mum about his parents, about how hard it had been for them, with their daughter's illness and then the SS requisitioning parts of their property. His father, he knew, was sometimes ill-tempered, but he was nevertheless a good, proud man who lamented his loss of independence and worried day and night about the precariousness of his position, knowing that if his secret guests were to be discovered, it would be the end for them, for him, for his family and for the whole village.

Such heart-warming words from this kind young man lifted Mum's spirits no end and came at a pivotal moment when all hope had seemed shattered to smithereens. We dusted ourselves off as much as possible and found a quiet spot away from the doors to sit and wait. When night fell, we were escorted into the Yakimchuks' home. I remember how blissful it was to feel the warmth of the house and to have generous amounts of water to drink, for a change; it was such a contrast to the brutal and spartan conditions in our pit, and unimaginably comforting after our unscheduled encounter with that brainless but unfortunate horse.

Mr Yakimchuk produced a big ladder for us to climb up into the rafters. My brothers were the first to ascend; but then came the troublemaker. My feet were too small, and negotiating the rickety ladder was very challenging. So Haim came back down, lifted me onto his back, and the two of us safely reached the summit. What a space. And no stinking buckets of shit.

Mum was the last to climb, and it took her a while as she was gasping for air. Her chest was giving up on her. When she finally reached the top, she collapsed on the wooden floor and begged for a moment of peace.

That new space was so welcome to us all. We could stretch our aching limbs and breathe in the fresh smell of hay.

Just as we had begun to feel safe and comfortable, we heard someone new come into the house. It was a boy, full of life and quite boisterous, as lads of his age will be. We later learned that he was Yakimchuk's nephew. In a loud voice, this visitor proclaimed, 'You lot are harbouring Jews.'

Mr Yakimchuk asked, 'Who told you that?'

'What do you mean?' the boy replied. 'I could see them with my own eyes.'

In the hush that filled the Yakimchuks' abode, we could sense that a new disaster was unfolding. But Mum's strength was evaporating rapidly, and she really couldn't take any more in.

'Now listen, Symon,' said Mr Yakimchuk, grabbing the boy hard.

The lad gave out a scream of pain. 'You are hurting me.'

'It will hurt even more if I hear you uttering another word to anyone. If you do, we are all finished. And you must especially not say a word to your mother, because she is the biggest gossip in the whole world. She will be the first to spread the news.'

The boy promised to keep the secret. The following morning, Mrs Yakimchuk took Symon to the priest to reaffirm his vow – this time in front of an icon – that he would never reveal his secret.

What a chain of events! One disaster after another. But at least it gave us all a brief respite in the attic. The space gave my brothers a good opportunity to walk about a bit, but the attic floor was not the most robust. Although the Yakimchuks warned us to be as quiet as possible, and not to move about on the shaky floorboards, the boys weren't as careful as they should have been. Meanwhile Mum's health was so poor at this time that she lacked the strength to control them. In reality, their high spirits were completely natural for boys of that age, but this was not a normal situation, and we were supposed to remain silent, despite having more space in this attic than we had experienced for a very long time.

On the Sunday, our peaceful interlude in the attic got even better for Haim and Shalom when they decided to dip into Mr Yakimchuk's store of apples and pears, resulting in quite a sugar rush that sent them prancing around. Meanwhile, the family had invited some people back to their house after church. Mr Yakimchuk was very generous with his home-brew, and the old lady served some of her best fare to the guests. The party was going on merrily, the adults seemingly too happy to stop the children being particularly boisterous. There was a lot of singing, and it all became very loud. We knew the Yakimchuks liked to entertain their guests, but all the whooping and jumping from below sounded a bit out of control and very out of character. Still, life is bleak enough, so why not let your hair down when there is an opportunity? The festivities went on well into the evening, and we heard a lot of glasses clinking in toasts, wishing '*Na zdorovie*' – Good health.

It got quite late before the last guest finally left and the front door was firmly shut. The Yakimchuks could breathe again. But not for long. We could hear the ladder being brought to the attic, and we were hoping that we might be about to be fed some of the leftovers.

Mrs Yakimchuk climbed up to us looking furious, which was so out of character, and she didn't keep her feelings to herself. She was very stern.

'Why did you make such a racket up here? We could hear all the commotion downstairs. Our guests kept asking, what is that noise coming from above? The old man wasn't able to stop for a moment, filling their glasses with his special *samagon* to make them drunk, so they would think the noise was all in their sozzled minds. We had to thump our feet and encourage the children to run wild. What would have happened if one of our friends had climbed up to the attic and seen you? What do you think the result would have been? It would have been the end of us all. How irresponsible! We are trying our best, under the most dangerous conditions, and you haven't given a scrap of thought to what the outcome of your bad behaviour might be.'

I wanted to say that it was the floorboards' fault, not ours, but I was too frightened.

Mum was lying on the floor, hardly breathing. She had a huge bump on her head, courtesy of the horse's hooves. She just listened to Mrs Yakimchuk's tirade, without saying a word. Normally, Mum's lack of a response might have infuriated the old lady, but now it was a moment when silence spoke louder than words.

When Mrs Yakimchuk got back down to the bottom of the ladder, her husband was waiting to question her about what our response had been. She didn't answer at first, but he persisted. When she still remained silent, he lost his temper and shook her by the shoulders.

'Why did they make such a racket? What was the reason?'

The old man's wife screwed up her lips as if saying, 'They said nothing.'

'What? They said nothing?' said the old man. 'They didn't apologize?'

'*Nichoho* [nothing],' was Mrs Yakimchuk's abrupt answer. The atmosphere in the house was starting to get very heated.

From then on we felt very much *personae non gratae* and just counted the minutes until we could vacate the attic. Maybe this wasn't Utopia after all.

At the crack of dawn, when the villagers were still asleep, we couldn't come down the ladder fast enough, even though we were still all badly wounded soldiers. Ivan came in, rubbing his palms together, full of pride at his great accomplishment:

'We have restored your pit and you can go back home. And you will be pleased to know the old horse has been fastened using a new, more robust rope.'

What a relief to be going 'home'. Suddenly the pit became almost tempting. My middle brother was first to descend from the attic, then my big brother. This time, he couldn't take me on his back, so I held on to him and, with deliberately slow steps, he managed to take me down. All of us were still peppered with bruises from our equine encounter, which had now turned black.

Then Haim went back to get Mum, who was very weak and could barely stand up. He did his best to encourage her: 'Please try, Mum. It won't be too long now before we can get back to Ludmir, we are almost there. Do it for us three.'

Even the aromatic smell of baking bread couldn't make us tarry a moment longer. Mum gathered herself, with Haim's help, and lowered herself down. She seemed so fragile that, with every step she made, we feared we might be witnessing the last of her. The human heart can bear only so much. Our farewell to the attic and its rickety floorboards was not particularly fond.

Even though the stopover in the Yakimchuks' house had been very brief, it proved to be really damaging in terms of trust and morale. It created an atmosphere of discord between us and the couple, and just now the chasm seemed unbridgeable. Mr Yakimchuk became rather distant with us. And although Mrs Yakimchuk kept replenishing the tunnel with potatoes, '*Bida, bida*' was seldom heard these days. We missed their visits and news from the outside world. We liked to be engaged with their daily lives. At times, their bulletins had been harrowing, especially when Otto Wächter's gang was on the prowl. Occasionally, however, there were events to cheer us, as when General Zhukov pulled out his best *Katyushas* (rocket launchers) and made sizeable gains.

But in truth, we were now a broken lot. Mum had suffered most injuries from the horse as she held us under her body to protect us from the thrashing hooves. When we had lowered ourselves once more into our newly restored grave, Ivan covered the top with a lid of branches and twigs. We were home at last.

The following day, Mr Yakimchuk came, though it was very much not in a spirit of reconciliation. He hadn't got over our eventful stay in his attic, and we knew that the revellers had come back the following day, just to see if the commotion in the attic was in their *samagon*-soaked imaginations or there really had been a racket from above. He assured them that it was the drink, which was a trifle more potent than his usual brew. He even put up his ladder. 'Please, go up and look for yourself. Nobody – nothing – there.' A few more toasts and a few more, '*Na zdorovie*'s and their doubts were banished. They returned home, reassured that it was all just a figment of their intoxicated imaginations.

We now anticipated what Mr Yakimchuk was going to say to us. That we had stretched his hospitality to its limits, and that it was high time for us to find new lodgings. That he had had quite enough of our damaged selves, and didn't want any more of our influence rubbing off on his family. We had out-stayed our welcome.

Mum, however, didn't give him an opportunity to start on a litany of complaints. She took the initiative at once. She told him that no one, even in his ghastliest nightmare, could have foreseen that the war would last this long after the Battle of Stalingrad ended in February 1943, but since it was still going on she could quite see that she and her children had outstayed his more than generous welcome and that it was now time to go. Maybe, she suggested, it would be a good idea to speak to

Ribke again, to see if he had any thoughts about where her family might safely go next.

The old man nodded as if engaged with what Mum was saying. It was a very solemn pitch by her. And then he replied as follows:

'You, at times, are like all women [he was a bit of a male chauvinist] who do not see the entire picture. You are asking me to speak to Ribke, who originally dropped me into the mess in which I now find myself. And you think he will have the right solution. Well, I am old enough and bruised enough by the ravages of war not to ask that idiot for any more advice. Look, the war has not yet finished; it's going the Soviets' way, but we aren't there yet. Do you imagine I'm so heartless that I would let the children go? Now? At times, events have a habit of knocking us sideways. We have been through so much together. But we dug you in, and we dug you out. And I have no doubt there will be more obstacles along the treacherous way ahead to try our patience and endurance. But one day this war will be over and until then we will persevere.'

Mum could scarcely believe what she was hearing; she was overwhelmed. Mr Yakimchuk was so unpredictable; you never knew what his next move would be. This time, however, he really focused on things affecting our position.

'The *buran* [blizzard] is calming, the barn isn't swaying as much so, with luck, it will survive the winter. The Germans are nowhere to be seen at the moment. They are all away, fighting their losing war. The Ukrainian collaborators, unfortunately, are still about. We can still hear them bragging about how many Jews they came across. But it sounds fewer and fewer, as not many are left for them to kill. They will outdo themselves with their zeal.'

While we were deep in conversation with the old man, we could hear footsteps. '*Bida, bida.*' Mrs Yakimchuk was back, bearing a pot of fresh water and a big fresh loaf of bread.

'Is that a house-warming gift?' Mum asked.

'Well,' she said, 'we could have had a party if my husband had thought to remove the pail of shit.'

We all laughed and Mum handed the aromatic pail to Mr Yakimchuk, who couldn't wait to get rid of its fine fragrance.

It was so great to see the two of them in good humour when they had every right to tell us to leave. We broke the bread and passed some to our host. It was quite a party. And as soon as they left, our childish imaginations kicked in and we envisioned our co-tenants, the mice, joining our soirée.

Chapter 12

Knitted Together

The tedium of time crawling aimlessly at an unhurried pace can undermine even the most resolute determination. By now, it was coming up to the best part of three months since we had first taken up lodgings in our dark, frozen pit, where the endless days were now chipping away at all thoughts of hope or purpose or future. The liberation of Kiev in late 1943 and Mr Yakimchuk's talk of Vatutin had given us so much encouragement to carry on, notwithstanding the overwhelming odds against our survival. It gave us hope that sometime soon we could be released from this fearful and circumscribed existence and yet, here we were still.

It began to play upon my middle brother's mind. His alter ego, Schpitalner Mensch, who had hitherto been happily at large and roaming freely in the world, was now back with us and planning to dig a tunnel all the way to Kiev.

Mum was beside herself: Shalom was her greatest worry, a bright boy with a hugely vivid imagination. She decided not to stop him from dreaming, since dreams were all he had; and yet, at the same time, she was not going to allow his creative inspiration to tip over into insanity. So she decided to indulge his fantasy world a little and she said to him: 'You know your friend? The one who's going to dig a tunnel. I'm sure he's very good with a shovel, but perhaps he's not so familiar with the terrain above. And he can't have any knowledge about the required distances, so you'll have to guide him along the way.' Mum gave him the names of the towns that would lead him to Kiev, along with their approximate distances from Biscobich, the starting point and the centre of our universe. Shalom would first need to direct Schpitalner Mensch to our home city, approximately fifteen kilometres away. When he left Volodymyr-Volynskyi, he would need time to reach Kovel, which was about fifty kilometres away. Mum would stretch all the distances for him in order to keep him fully occupied. Then, he would have to give his mate a break, as he'd be tired from digging. The earth was frozen solid and it was back-breaking labour.

Then, suddenly Shalom said: 'Mum, Kovel will be dangerous for my friend. A lot of German soldiers are out there. He won't be safe.'

Mum was happy that her son was still making lucid points. She said: 'Being underground, nobody would guess that some creature was hiding below.'

'Yes, Mum. Just like us now.'

Schpitalner Mensch had to go to Lutsk. It didn't take him too long, as he'd had a rest and gathered his strength. 'Now Mum, what's going to happen to the soil that was dug above?

A photograph of my mother, Rivka Akin, and father, Moshe Fischmann, taken for their engagement. The photographs on this page were sent to family in Newcastle before the war, which is why they survived.

My father in one of his kayaks on the River Lug. His brother Joel is in the water.

From left to right: my mother Rivka and father Moshe, Grandma Miriam,
Uncle Hirsch and his wife, and Uncle Joel.

This photograph of Jewish survivors from Volodymyr-Volynskyi was taken at
Piatydni, not long before we left. I am the little girl sitting by the marker, Haim is
lying on the other side, and my mother is leaning on the stone.

Mr Yakimchuk and his grandson. It is thanks to the brave Yakimchuks, who hid us for nine months, that we survived the final liquidation of the ghetto.

The only surviving photo of Mrs Yakimchuk.
I've never forgotten her smiling face.

Mr and Mrs Yakimchuk's son, Ivan.

Ivan and his wife Manka.
Two of the children are
Stefan and Alexandra,
I believe.

Myself aged eight with
Mum and Shalom at the
DP camp in Italy.

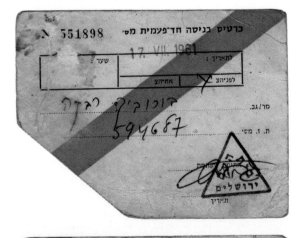

My mum's ticket for the trial
of Adolf Eichmann. The ticket
is stamped 17 July 1961.

With David at the Grand Hotel in Lviv on our visit in 1997.

Symon, who found out that the Yakimchuks were hiding us but kept our secret as a little boy.

Arriving at the station in Volodymyr-Volynskyi and being reunited with Alexandra and Stefan.

I'm sitting next to Alexandra, with David and Stefan behind us, in a coach
on our way to meet up with Symon.

Reunited for a wonderful dinner. On the left is David and Alexandra,
I am in the middle, and Stefan and his wife are on the right.

Monument to the victims of the Nazis in Piatydni.

Sitting at my dining room table and working on this book during the Covid pandemic.

The Germans will become suspicious when they see all the earth.'

'Yes, that's quite a problem,' said Mum. 'Now look, why don't you direct your man to go through the forest. There he'll find friendly partisans. They may even give him a crust of bread.'

'Mum, what a great idea. I like the forest. He might even pick some berries and mushrooms.'

Suddenly, big brother Haim joined in. 'You twit! Foraging in the winter when the forest is frozen! Don't kid yourself: the Polish partisans will soon kill him, just like the people from the ghetto who tried to hook on to them.'

Mum quickly intervened. 'So how far are we now? How many kilometres have we completed?'

Big brother stuck his oar in again: 'You mean "How many has he achieved?" He's still in Biscobich, and there are still four hundred and fifty kilometres to Kiev.'

'You might be in Biscobich. You don't have a friend to dig for you! I'm on my way to see Chernobyl; and next week, I'll be in Korosten. And then, I'll be in Zhytomyr. And then Berdychiv.'

'We had some family in Berdychiv,' Mum said. 'I shudder to think what happened to them.'

By the time he got to Korosten, he'd run out of towns, and the digging stretched on to an empty, frozen infinity. Whenever I remind Shalom of his imaginary friend he howls with laughter. It's one of the few memories he can bear to relive. After the war we never spoke of it in front of Mum, though; she found it too upsetting.

With all the tunnels theoretically dug and the distances

calculated, Mum began to worry that Haim might be getting jealous that she was giving so much attention to her younger son. She was afraid that big brother's imagination might also start planning a disturbing new escape of its own. He was not a daydreamer and his inventive mind made the threat of his running away very real.

An idea of absolute genius then occurred to her, in order to nip any such thoughts in the bud. When the Yakimchuks' daughter-in-law appeared with the black, chipped pot of water, Mum asked: 'Manka, do you by any chance possess some knitting needles?'

Thinking it was a joke, Manka started laughing. 'Who's going to knit and where's the wool coming from?'

Mum assured her that she would find some wool and that all she needed were some needles.

On Sunday, before church, Manka appeared, all dolled up – bright lipstick, beautiful vibrant scarf on her head, body enclosed in a chequered wrap – complaining: 'What a *buran*! I wonder if many people will come to the service.'

She fished out from under her arm a bundle wrapped in yellow cloth, handed it to Mum and giggled.

'I had to be careful with this parcel of needles. If I was caught, I couldn't say it was for the dog, could I.'

That made everyone laugh. Manka had such a full, healthy, rich laugh; alas, a sound that seldom emanated from our dwelling. She then left for church, no doubt wondering what fate awaited those rusty needles.

When Mum unwrapped the bundle, she was astonished to see the collection that Manka had managed to put together.

And she announced, 'We are going to knit.' Now, since my middle brother was aware that, thanks to the efforts of his alter ego, his tunnel had already just about reached its intended destination, and my big brother was feeling excited just at the thought of making himself a pullover that would keep him warm on his own escaping forays, both of them seemed ready and eager to embark on this new venture. And so was I; indeed, we all embraced the endeavour with an ardent passion.

Mum took off the large brown cardigan that had kept the harsh elements away and began unpicking its wool. And in conjunction with the boys, a production line was soon established. Mum was the 'unpicker'; my big brother was the 'gatherer', who put the yarn into bundles. Then I stretched my arms out to their full extent so that the unpicked wool could be wound round them in strands, before my middle brother rolled it into neat balls of yarn, ready for our needles. Needless to say, without my brilliant and crucial effort, production would never have taken off.

Next, it was the turn of the rusty needles. The boys were enthusiastically polishing them; they applied a layer of rough soil (a commodity in considerable abundance right on our doorstep), rubbing it up and down the needles vigorously, then shined them to a polish with the cloth that Mrs Yakimchuk had originally wrapped them in. Though I tried my hand at polishing, my clever brother said I was rubbish, which earned him a punch on the nose from my big brother. When the victim looked to Mum for sympathy, she just said: 'Serves you right.'

When Haim was almost finished polishing his needles, he gave them to me for a final, expert rub. I took pride in making them as shiny as I possibly could, much to Shalom's annoyance.

Now the needles were ready and, thanks to our group efforts, the balls of yarn were also prepared. So, all was now ready for the master knitter to begin her opening lecture. My brothers took to this new task like ducks to water; and, with a fair amount of tutoring and unpicking and picking, of mistakes, they produced two sleeveless pullovers. They might have been sweaters with long sleeves, but alas, the wool ran out.

Mum devised such a practical and potentially life-saving distraction for her children all the while knowing she would be exposing herself to the bitter conditions without her large brown cardigan.

Mr Yakimchuk came to the barn with some produce for Prisoner Number Five. We could all overhear his long heart-to-heart with his friend, once again pouring out his grievances. This time, it was mainly about oven smoke filling the house. He said, 'The wood's so wet and refuses to burn', while he busily rubbed the soot out of his eyes and expected at the very least some sympathy. But the horse just crunched away on a heap of carrots and drank the well water.

'Well done, old boy,' said Mr Yakimchuk, and we could hear him muttering away about the injustices of life while gathering up a pile of the horse's manure with his big fork.

Mr Yakimchuk's next port of call was our aromatic pail. Poor man. He really did not deserve that particular chore. Mum tried to engage him in conversation, but he was not in a chatty mood. His eyes were bright red and tears were streaming down his face. Mum said, 'Yakimchuk, it looks like you had a late night, judging by the state of your eyes.'

'I wish! I cleaned all the soot from the oven, much to my wife's delight. You should have seen it. It was as good as when I first built it. But now we've used up all the dry wood to keep Paraska warm. She's very ill. And all that's left to burn are the wet stumps. It's a devil to get the flame going.'

Mum greatly sympathized with the old man, while handing over the pail of shit to him. 'I'm so sorry for all you are going through. I'm sure your hero, Vatutin, will soon bring the war to an end.'

'Woman, now you are talking! Nikolai will do it.'

Mum knew the man so well and managed to put him in a much finer frame of mind. He had loved his time as a soldier in the First World War. It filled him with pride, and his medals were testimony to his achievements. This briefly made him forget all about the smoke and the oven. Even the pail of shit was smelling sweeter.

When Mr Yakimchuk came back with the emptied bucket, he looked at my big brother. 'What is that you are wearing?'

'Do you mean my pullover? I knitted it,' Haim said proudly.

'Really?' said Mr Yakimchuk. 'I heard from Manka about the knitting campaign, I was sure it was a joke'.

'No, it was not. I did it with my own two hands and two needles.'

The old man was astonished. 'Capital, capital, young man.'

'This pullover is going to keep me warm when I escape from here.'

The old man laughed, 'Tell me when, I'll come with you.'

Normally, Mr Yakimchuk would have had baked potatoes in his pocket; but for some reason this time there were none to be had. When he left us, I aired my disappointment about their non-appearance, but clever brother soon came out with, 'You are an idiot! How could he bring potatoes when the wood's not burning? There's no coal for baking.'

The next day, '*Bida, bida*' was echoing in the distance. Yes, it was Mrs Yakimchuk approaching in her snug felt boots. She was looking very anxious, and we gathered from the tone of her voice that she was quite agitated. Mum said, 'We saw Mr Yakimchuk yesterday, and he was telling us about the oven that refuses to get going. It must be quite a problem without the heat, especially as the frost is getting worse by the minute.'

Mrs Yakimchuk looked at Mum with a very sad demeanour and said: 'I wish it was only the oven, which, as you say, is essential; but we were up most of the night with Paraska. She is fading away. When I leave you, I'm going to see the priest. I still have a couple of rings to give him for the church. I'm sure he will put in a few good words for our daughter.'

Mum felt so deeply for this pious woman and her very poorly daughter. She commiserated and dearly wished she could be of some help. Mrs Yakimchuk's hands were trembling out of worry, as a ferocious storm howled outside around the barn. She lowered the basin of mash into the pit, along with a stale loaf of bread, dotted with green mouldy spots. This was the best she could find for us, until the wood eventually dried out and the oven could again function at full blast.

Mrs Yakimchuk walked away, stooped in sadness. '*Bida, bida*', that melancholy call of 'misfortune', was reverberating louder than ever. Mum felt so helpless. If only she could do something to help save Paraska. She could imagine the sorrow of watching one's child fade away, the desperate worry when her health became worse, the hope that came every time Paraska seemed to improve. It must have been exhausting.

We didn't indulge in Mrs Yakimchuk's gastronomic offerings straight away. We waited for a little bit until she had replaced the twigs, which took more time than usual as her acutely painful situation was draining her strength. Then, the boys dug into their cold mash with their hands since, by now, our spoons had succumbed to metal fatigue and snapped.

This dilemma raised the fiddly question of how to mend our broken utensils. The fragile handles were now clearly beyond repair; but the bowls of the spoons, though far from perfect, were nevertheless salvageable. So, the boys agreed to a compromise solution: the spoon bowls would remain, but the handles would be replaced with wooden stems. The snag here was finding a way to attach the new stems to the original bowls. But this difficulty was soon overcome by our genius-in-residence. Mum produced a bit of wool left over from our recent knitting campaign, using that to entwine the new, perfectly carved wooden handles to the bowls. A marriage made in Biscobich.

Chapter 13

Kovel

The Germans were back in the cowshed, preparing their horses and equipment. This was probably March 1944 but I can't be more exact. We believed they must have been on their way to Kovel, a city that was to occupy our anxious thoughts for months.

At this time along the Eastern Front, the opposing armies had reached deadlock. The Germans were desperate to keep the Soviets at bay until spring arrived. Another winter in Russia would have been the end of them, so they were essentially just playing for time. But Stalin had time on his side, and he had the manpower. He poured millions of people in.

Kovel, which was held by the Germans, had an important road junction and was effectively the barrier between East and West. If it could gain control of Kovel, the Red Army would be on the road to Berlin – stopping first to liberate us, we hoped.

When he was able to visit us, Mr Yakimchuk told us that the Soviets had attacked Kovel the day before (on 17 March according to the history books) and the fighting was fierce. The Germans in Kovel would need reinforcements to hold out.

While the men in the cowshed worked, they chanted at the tops of their voices: '*Wenn Judenblut vom Messer spritzt, dann freuen wir uns und lachen wir uns* [When Jewish blood spurts from our knife, then we rejoice and laugh].'

Quite a chorus to reach the ears of three small frozen, frightened, hungry and thirsty children. I later discovered that this had also been the Nazis' boating song when they'd gone out joyriding in my dad's kayaks. My brothers remembered this tune only too well.

Our current position was as desperate as it had ever been – both for us and the Yakimchuks. Occasionally they managed to throw some potatoes through the tunnel guarded by the inquisitive dog, but water became very scarce and so thirst was our biggest issue. It was difficult for Mrs Yakimchuk to come to us with the black chipped pot of water. And although the cold was getting less biting, which was a blessing, there was now no ice to quench our thirst. When Mr Yakimchuk came to bring some water for Prisoner Number Five, we were deliriously happy to have a sip or two.

The previous order that had guided our lives was beginning to collapse. My brother the escape plotter had had enough. He was more and more desperate to break out of our putrefying grave. Mum was getting weaker by the day, with the responsibility of looking after three small children starting to seriously take its toll. She was worn out emotionally, and increasingly fragile. The beating inflicted by Zavidovich in the ghetto, the concussion inflicted by the Polish policeman who'd struck her with his pistol when he was denied the chance to shoot her, her crushing encounter with Mr Yakimchuk's horse, the almost total lack of nourishment – all these torments came at a cost to her physically, a cost that left her suffering for the rest of her life. Her chest at times sounded like an orchestra tuning up. She was drained.

Looking after three children in such a confined and dark space presented its own constant challenge. But up to now, she had muddled through. She always had to listen to Mr Yakimchuk very carefully; at the same time, she never appeared to be a weak woman, and she always retained her pride. Even our pit was swept daily with a little broom she made of twigs and we always had to leave a few drops of water in the pot so she could wash the bowl that held the mash before returning it to Mrs Yakimchuk. I think it was very astute of Yakimchuk to see from the start that she was no pushover, something he found very endearing at times. She even made him laugh when the situation was completely beyond irony.

One symptom of Mum's decline was her increasingly frequent tendency to doze off. It was during one of these brief absences that Haim seized the moment for his great escape.

Unobserved, he crawled out from the pit and into the barn, where he remained for several hours. Then, suddenly, in a state of abject fear, he jumped into the pit and told Mum that a German had seen him and was going to come back with his gun and shoot us all. Half-awake and disoriented, Mum was stunned, but took it all very seriously. If the story had come from Shalom, she might have dismissed it out of hand, since he was known for his vivid imagination. But Haim was more down-to-earth and prosaic; historically, tall tales had played no part in his repertoire.

He told Mum we must flee at once. She asked, 'Are you sure it was not a dream? You know, the fresh air in the barn might have made you drowsy and you could have fallen asleep, which would be understandable, after breathing all the stifling air in here and the stink from the bucket. It's not the best place to have a decent nap. And I'm sure I would have woken up at once if any German had talked to you – my ears are always attuned to any new sound.'

'No, Mum, we must go before the German comes back. He went to get soldiers and weapons.'

'What, for a miserable lot like us? He would not need more soldiers.'

Haim's conviction was very persuasive, but Mum wasn't sure what to believe. So she said, 'If we go out, Germans will be all over the yard. What a trophy they'll be getting. And we must think about the Yakimchuks. If we're caught, the future for them is not going to be pretty. Nor for the village, not to mention the priest. It's going to be Armageddon here. So, I think we must just sit and wait. Whatever you think, it might still have been a dream. Think about it logically. If the German really saw you, the first thing he would have done would have been to go and see Yakimchuk. And he would have been here in a flash. And if not him, then somebody from the family. But nobody has appeared, which is a positive sign. So, let's not make any decisions in haste. Trying to escape now would be the worst option, because we'd be caught in no time. No, we just have to sit and wait to see what's going to pan out.'

'You're making the wrong decision, Mum,' Haim said urgently.

'You know, son, at times you have to go with your gut feeling, which means we just have to stay put. The best idea is for you to stop escaping.'

And so we sat, ears straining to hear any sound, waiting for discovery and death, a wait that seemed to be stretching to eternity. Eventually, that evening, Mr Yakimchuk appeared, carrying a pail of water for his horse. We couldn't wait to put our heads in the pail to quench our choking thirst. The farmer was in a good mood: he announced that his oven was back at full blast and that Mrs Yakimchuk was on her way with a fresh loaf of bread.

Clearly the German was no more than a fearful dream. The tragedy was that we were now struggling to distinguish between reality and fantasy.

After all the devastation that the Germans had inflicted on western Russia and Ukraine, the Soviets were now retaliating with – if anything – even greater ferocity.

It was now about four months since we had first come to Biscobich and started languishing in our underground, godforsaken living hell. In our pit, we were desperate for the Soviets to crank up the conflict. They held the key to setting us free from our tenuous, barbaric existence. 'Existence': even that word would be an overstatement – we were worn down, broken emotionally and physically. We were frozen, we had very little food, we were frightened to be seen and terrified of even our own shadows. I said to Mum, 'How lucky the horses in the field are. At least they have water to drink.' She burst into tears and I felt very guilty and wished I'd never opened my big mouth.

We hadn't heard from the Yakimchuks for a whole day, and I was asking Mum, 'Where's my bread?' I glanced at my brothers' faces which, for once, didn't look sheepish. And my friends the mice were nowhere to be seen. I couldn't understand why the bread wasn't there. I then repeated my question more forcefully: 'Where is the bread and where are the mice?'

My brothers, who didn't have much time for me, thought it a particularly stupid thing to say. 'You are brainless. There aren't any mice because there isn't any bread.'

'Well,' I asked them, 'what is going to happen with no bread?'

'The same as is happening to our souls,' they replied, enigmatically. But then they added: 'The Yakimchuks will be here soon, and we will have a feast.'

But the Yakimchuks did not appear. Mum kept us in check by telling us stories from our past. There was a limit to Mum's supply of family stories, which meant we would hear them over and over again. She would recall the times we visited our grandparents on their farm, and remind us of when our father used to race his bike, or about when Grandpa Akin fell out of his sleigh. When snow was thick on the ground, Grandpa's wagon would be swapped for a sleigh pulled by a horse. On this particular day, one of Grandpa's labourers was driving while Grandpa rested. He was wrapped up warmly in his furs, lulled by the swoosh of the runners and the jingle of the harness, and had fallen fast asleep. At some point the driver had turned to talk to him and was astonished to find Grandpa gone. Hurriedly turning back, he found his bewildered employer lying in a snowbank on the side of the road. He was completely unharmed but as grumpy as a bear disturbed in winter.

We now knew these stories by heart. Me and my big, clever brothers.

Both my brothers had good educations before we were locked down in the ghetto; they went to private schools. I never admitted how inferior to them I felt.

The boys were becoming very agitated, as life became more and more tedious. My brother the escapee was again planning a bid for freedom, but Mum caught him just in time. This was all quite a struggle for her; a major headache. When night fell, she took a basin and crawled out from the pit into the barn itself. There, she gathered handfuls of snow and ice and crawled back in, so at least our thirsts were quenched.

A day later, we three children developed coughs, but nothing serious. Mum, on the other hand, took ill in a very bad way. She had a high fever and a horrendous hacking cough. She could hardly breathe. She looked as if she was fading away in front of our eyes. The following day, her condition worsened. She tried not to cough, but she ended up choking and pointing to her chest. We needed to let her cough properly, but at the same time keep the noise to a minimum so she would not be heard outside the pit. As soon as her coughing fits started, all three of us had to pile on top of her head to deaden the sound. Mum was left gasping for air.

We were now in the most appalling situation, but had still heard no word from the Yakimchuks. On the one hand we felt completely abandoned, and yet on the other we were obviously very concerned about whatever it was that might have happened to them. This was surely one of the lowest moments of our confinement there. We were totally lost – we had no father, and now Mum looked as if she would soon be joining him. She was so weak. She had stopped talking and had lost every last vestige of strength. We put up with this desperate decline for three days; on the morning of the fourth day, Mum looked as if she was close to death.

About mid-morning, Ivan's wife Manka finally appeared. When she saw the state Mum was in, she was utterly horrified. It transpired that the snow had been so bad, it had blocked the Yakimchuks' front door. They had been trapped in the house, unable to open the door and escape. Ivan, the Yakimchuks' son, was away, digging trenches for the Germans, and there was no one else to help dig them out. The old man had had to do it all himself, but in the process he too had fallen ill. It was also too dangerous to try to bring us any food, since German troops were passing through the village on their way to Kovel, where the battle continued to rage. The Yakimchuks were just too scared, both for themselves and for us.

The situation was now extremely difficult. And it was made worse when Manka told us that somebody knew of a family in a village nearby who had been harbouring Jewish people. The

Gestapo had been informed, and the Jewish people discovered and killed, and the entire village had been obliterated as punishment. This event had shaken the Yakimchuk household to the core. We were appalled. It seemed highly likely that we would soon be discovered as well. Although this possibility had been ever-present in all our minds since the day we had entered our pit, the thought that detection was now potentially so close shook us rigid. It was the very last thing we wanted to hear. It would also give the old man every reason to return with his map, and if he'd decided that this time we really must leave, it would have been very hard to blame him.

The only remaining question now was the logistics, finding a safe way forward. I have no doubt that Mr Yakimchuk, who would have had time to contemplate this new state of affairs while ill in bed, would be coming up with a plan. Meanwhile Manka, sighing heavily and with head bowed, looked at Mum with enormous sympathy.

Gasping deeply, and pointing to her aching chest, Mum pleaded with Manka:

'You can see that I am fading,' she told her. 'Somehow, I must keep going. You can help me, if only for my children's sake. If you could bring me a pot of hot water and some dry camomile, I will inhale it and it will help my breathing. That was a potion that my mother used to concoct. Mum would swear by it.'

Manka looked hesitant, in view of all the dangers outside, but the expression on her face told Mum that she would try. She said: 'I'll do my utmost. But the hot water's going to be a challenge. When people see me with food and cold water, I say I'm taking it for the dog. I know these villagers are not overburdened with brains, but even they can get suspicious. They might ask, "What, hot water for the dog! Are you trying to kill him?"'

As a thank you, Mum took off her wedding ring, that precious link with Dad, and gave it to Manka who put it on her finger; it fitted perfectly. She promised Mum she would do what she could and left in a hurry, admiring her present.

At sunset we heard that heavy tread, swaying from side to side, as if going through choppy waters (and these waters could not have been choppier). We heard '*Bida, bida*', a mournful sound that nevertheless filled our souls with hope as it meant help was coming from Mrs Yakimchuk. She came in with a large vessel full of hot boiling water filled with dried camomile flowers. The smell alone could awaken a corpse. When she saw the state Mum was in, she fell to the ground asking, 'Why? Who was so heartless to bring us to such a hopeless situation?' Of course, no one had an answer. Mrs Yakimchuk then put her hand in her pocket and passed over Mum's wedding ring, apologizing on Manka's behalf.

'You know what young people today are like. They don't understand what life is about.'

Mum took the pot of hot water from Mrs Yakimchuk's burning hands, lowered her head towards the perfumed brew and covered herself with the tattered blanket. When she lifted her head from this magical potion, her breathing was so much better and she could speak. Mrs Yakimchuk said that she had found a locket that Mum had slipped in her pocket when we all met at Ribke's. She was going to donate it to the church and get the priest to pray for Mum.

After several more camomile-scented bowls, each brought to the accompaniment of '*Bida, bida*', Mum slowly started to improve.

Chapter 14

Passover 1944

As March turned to April the days got longer and less cold, but the cold gave way to more rain; snow and ice still lingered, and there would be fresh snowfalls before the winter finally passed. The monotony of life was getting even harder. Our limbs felt as if they didn't really belong to us. My legs started to bend inwards. Mum's beautiful legs swelled up, and my middle brother could hardly stand. The only one who was almost entirely unscathed was Haim. That might have been because he had to stay fit for his planned 'escapes'.

In the evenings, Mum would sit at the edge of the pit to stretch her legs, always ready to jump back in if she heard a strange noise. Her main entertainment was listening to the frogs croaking. They seemed to be enjoying themselves, and it made a nice change from the tedium of our living grave.

In the mornings, Mrs Yakimchuk would come and tell us what she'd heard in church: lots of gossip, none of it malicious. She loved her precious time with the priest, who would complain about his flock, saying, 'So few are coming to his services these days, the confession box is empty. Not that their lives are free from sin, but the war took away the men, and the ladies have very shallow pockets.'

She was looking forward to better days. 'And soon it will be Easter' – as she mentioned Easter her face lit up – 'and we will have *babka* [sweet braided bread] and *kulich* [Russian Easter bread]. And we will decorate eggs, which is very time-consuming, yet so beautiful and festive.'

'It sounds so promising and joyful,' Mum said. She so wished she could take part in the preparations, but of course she could not come out of our hideaway and risk discovery. But it struck me that even talking about normal life was something of a solace for her, and I noticed that war was no longer top of either woman's agenda.

Mrs Yakimchuk soon had to rush back to the house, which was such a shame. That old lady had a wonderfully melodic voice. We always hoped that one day when she graced us with her company – perhaps even the next time – her '*Bida, bida*' would be replaced by '*Slava*' (Glory).

At Kovel, the Germans had held out, and by early April the Red Army had stopped their ferocious attack. Suddenly, our freedom seemed further away than ever.

One day Mr Yakimchuk came to visit us and we noticed that he was not wearing his fur coat or the big hat that covered his ears. Instead, he had on a woollen hat and a padded jacket – his new outfit for the spring. He asked for the perfumed bucket, which we were so happy to bequeath to him; he even smiled as he took it. When he returned he sat down on the edge of our grace-and-favour home and began to speak. He seemed full of optimism.

'*Now*,' he said. Our ears pricked up. 'I hear that the Russians are still outside Kovel. They are not giving up. The German army may be hanging on for now but it's only a matter of time.'

At the time I didn't understand what this might mean. I was just about to ask Mr Yakimchuk where the baked potatoes were, but the old fox beat me to it. He pulled out a few from his pocket. I bet his wife was going to be cross with him for ruining his new spring outfit.

As Easter approached so did the Jewish Passover. Through the power of her storytelling, Mum transported us to Grandpa Akin's house in Lytovezh, where all the family would gather in happier days. And what a great time it had been for all the children, playing in the cherry orchard where white blossom garlanded the trees, fighting about whose turn it was to go in the hammock. Grandma Hannah would have been bustling around after preparing for months to feed the extended family. As Mum relived those times, she shed nostalgic tears (not too many, so that the sadness might not hit us too hard; as if we didn't have enough of that already). She just looked at us, as if to say, 'See what's left now, just the four of us, from such a big a family, once seventy-eight strong.'

She went on to tell us about how life had been before the war.

'All the family from Lemberg would descend,' Mum said. Mind you, there was a bit of jealousy going on, naturally. They were a sophisticated lot, coming from such a beautiful medieval city. It has so many fine buildings, a magnificent opera house, even a tram system. By comparison, we looked like country yokels. But Grandmother Hannah didn't like being outdone and would wear her rather large, chunky chain which was so long we warned her to take care not to trip over it. She would bedeck herself with her fine sparkly jewels; Grandpa Akin used to look at her with admiration. He didn't keep his dry sense of humour in his tallit bag. He would tease his wife, "Hannah, you look like a well-lit *yolka* [festive fir tree]."'

The boys found this rather funny and burst out laughing. 'Oh, Grandma Yolka.' I didn't quite get the joke, but I wasn't going to let them know I didn't understand the funny side of the story, so I just giggled.

'Grandma would say, "Well, Mr Akin, I have to make an effort. Look at the competition I'm up against. All these elegant Hapsburgers"

'Grandpa always had a new satin robe for high holidays, fastened by a shiny cord with tassels. And always a new white shirt from Warsaw, the metropolis of fine fashion, the Paris of Poland. There was a saying in our city, "Let it be shit as long as it's from Warsaw!" Anything that came from there had such panache. And then came Grandpa's *shtreimel*, an outsized hat made from shiny satin and trimmed with fur. My dad was a top man, so smart; he certainly knew how to make an entrance. He looked so imperial.

'Then your Aunt Fruma, who lived in Russia, would arrive. It was such a long journey that she could only come in the spring when the weather was pleasant, but it was so good to see her. Fruma always came bearing Russian gifts. Grandpa would bring out his best wagon, pulled by his finest stallion, to meet her at the station. It was such a warm reunion.

'Then, from America, my Uncle Moshe would arrive. He liked to be called Morris, his American name. He would stay with us since his parents had disowned him. When he first started out in life, he was a rabbi with a PhD and studied in Vilnius. After he qualified, he had a change of heart and wrote home saying that he couldn't see himself making a living from the Bible. When this bombshell landed at his parents' house, they sat shiva [a period of formal mourning when someone dies]. He was forbidden to come home, and so he fled to Vienna to study medicine. When he qualified as an ear, nose and throat consultant, he left for America. How lucky was he?

'Although some of our relatives deplored what Moshe had done, Grandpa always kept in touch with him and made him very welcome. It was such an honour to have a rabbi in the family. It was so great to have Uncle Moshe at the Seder table to begin Passover; it was such a joyous occasion. Your grandma would take out her best Rosenthal dinner service, with more gilding than the tsar's Winter Palace, which she kept just for Passover, along with the silver cutlery that Grandpa bought in Kiev. Then out would come the special silver charger, divided into compartments, to be filled with traditional bitter herbs and special nutty mincemeat. Each one represents a specific story from the time when we were slaves in Egypt. Grandpa would fish out the old Haggadah [the text setting out the order of Passover], which had lost much of its lustre and turned yellow, with some of its pages torn. It was hard to decipher, but Uncle Moshe knew the books by heart. Although he was no longer an observer of the faith, he still knew the meaning of every word. His Hebrew was perfect. Although the others were strict followers of the religion, they were clueless about the meaning of the sentences that were written in the book. Occasionally they became emotional and tearful when the sentence was really rather uplifting – such as when we had just left Egypt where we were slaves and now were free. Pesach is also called the Festival of Freedom.

'We all had to finish reading the whole book from cover to cover. Then came the singing of the traditional Jewish songs. Nobody was allowed to leave the table. It all had to strictly follow the ancient custom that was laden with tears and sorrow.

'Then came the children's turn. By that time, they were all so groggy and tired out, Grandpa would make an announcement: "Who has found the *afikoman* [piece of the matza]?" and suddenly all the children came to life to search for the elusive *afikoman*. And as you may guess, there were lots of *afikomans*, and most were discovered. At the end came the children's presents, followed by the toast: "Next year in Jerusalem".'

'Wow, Mum, what a story!'

It should have been bleak because of what later happened to our family, but Mum's story somehow raised our spirits, because it was confirmation that there had been another life, before the ghetto and the pit, and that raised the possibility that what once there had been might come again.

Chapter 15

Easter

So Passover was celebrated in our imaginations, and Easter was lived vicariously through the Yakimchuks. We heard more about the planning from Mr Yakimchuk, who settled down to tell us about all the Easter festivities; how busy his wife was with her hands deep in kneading dough, getting all the *babkas* and *kulichs* ready. The problem was that the bread was not rising well because yeast was in short supply.

Manka and her children were painting the *pysanky*, as the Easter eggs were called; the kitchen was overflowing with colourful dye. 'I even got it on my new coat,' he said, then added, 'Well, it is Easter. Let's be happy.'

'Oh yes,' Mum said. 'Mrs Yakimchuk will get rid of the stains.'

'I have full confidence in the old lady. Tomorrow is Easter Sunday and we all go to church. And then, my barrels will be cracked open.'

'Not too many, Yakimchuk,' said Mum. 'You will get a bad headache.'

He laughed so loudly he almost choked and said, 'Not as bad as you lot give me.' Then he replaced the dry twigs and went off to join the revellers.

At the crack of dawn on 16 April, much earlier than normal, Mrs Yakimchuk came, breathless and looking excited, carrying her large basket of plenty.

We noticed that she was wearing a new scarf. A big smile spread across her pious face, revealing a few gaps in her teeth. She was so delighted with that bright head-covering, its white fabric decorated with big red roses and foliage.

'This is for church,' she proudly proclaimed. She gingerly pushed the twigs to one side, lowered her basket down to us and said, 'This is for you for Easter. Don't be shy, open it.'

It didn't take too much encouragement for us to open the magic basket, which contained a feast fit for the tsar. *Babkas* and *kulichs* and beautifully coloured eggs. Fabergé, eat your heart out.

The excitement that infused our gloomy pit brought everything suddenly to life. We couldn't wait to start indulging in such fine fare. A sumptuous display like this was foreign to us as traditionally at this time we had dumplings and dry matzes.

Mum told us before we tucked in to the food that we must thank Mrs Yakimchuk for her great kindness. My vocabulary in Ukrainian was very limited, stretching no further than '*Pechery, kartopli*' ('Baked potatoes, please'), but there were none to be seen in that basket. Mum spoke Ukrainian very well, so she surely had many words to thank that good lady for her generosity and kindness; but most of all for her spirit.

Mrs Yakimchuk adjusted her beautiful new scarf with pride.

'Sorry, I have to dash before the church fills up. I always like to get a seat near the altar, especially at Easter. It gets crowded.'

We couldn't quite believe this was all real and actually happening: had Mr Yakimchuk slipped a few drops of his famous brew into our water? It took some time for that basket of plenty to finally lighten. When the last egg had been cracked and all the cake consumed, our co-dwellers, the mice, came to forage for crumbs. When every last speck was gone, they gracefully bowed out.

Manka came in the evening after church and replenished our black chipped pot with fresh water from the well. She looked so radiant and full of the joys of Easter, her skin as smooth as alabaster and her beautiful blonde hair plaited on the crown of her head, creating a golden tiara, entwined with a garland of flowers suspending long ribbons in vibrant colours. She wore a white blouse embroidered with red and black cross-stitching and her red satin skirt reached almost to the ground. All finished off with an embroidered half-apron tied to her small waist. What an ensemble. She was ready for the ball.

'You look so magnificent,' Mum said admiringly.

Manka giggled, her bright blue eyes dancing with glee. She couldn't stop for long. They were expecting Ribke to come and spend Easter with his uncle and aunt. Biscobich came alive whenever Easter approached. When Mum heard that Ribke was due to arrive, she smiled.

'We'd better hold tight. Turmoil is approaching. Manka, have you prepared the old man for the onslaught?'

'Well,' she said, 'almost. We left it to Ivan. Whenever we have heated arguments, we leave it to the peacemaker. Old Yakimchuk will just have to get over his anger. A few glasses of *samagon* will soon cure any rift. Oh, families, families.'

The Easter festivities were in full swing, with the villagers whole-heartedly singing their traditional Ukrainian songs. 'Such good pitch,' said Mum. The sound of happiness filled our souls with joy, such a complete contrast to our usual bleak existence. May Easter go on for a long, long time.

We were anxiously anticipating the arrival of Ribke, our knight in shining armour. It would be so nice to see another friendly face. We waited and waited, well into the night, but we didn't hear any unusual footsteps. However, in the far distance where the road ran between Ludmir and Kovel, what we did hear was choruses of '*Seig Heil*' and '*Deutschland über alles*', followed by the '*Königgrätzer Marsch*' (the Wehrmacht Victory March), which was a bit premature. Two choirs, singing from such different hymn sheets.

The following morning, we waited eagerly for Ribke's visit. It would be such a momentous reunion. There was so much to discuss: what might the future hold for us?

At that time, Mum was in her mid-thirties – what should have been the prime of life. But she was widowed, with three small children, no other remaining family nearby and no home. Her dark, sleek hair had gone white almost overnight, her big violet eyes were sunken and there was a sadness that never left her.

Mum was contemplating what would certainly be at the top of the agenda when Ribke appeared: finding a way to free the

Yakimchuk family from our presence here. No matter how careful we were not to be seen, our lives hung in the balance. And that balance rested in the hands of one young boy, who we were trusting not to disclose our existence, even accidentally. The mere fact of our presence here created such peril for so many.

Ribke came the following day. As he moved the twigs that covered our hiding place, the expression on his face told our story. He looked quite unprepared for the ageing woman and the three wretched children that confronted him. As he sat down at the edge of the pit, Mum said, 'Sorry, Ribke. This is the best seat in the house.' Ribke offered a friendly hand, as if to say, 'Well, you are still here.' The Yakimchuks were used to witnessing our worsening condition, but it must have been a devastating shock for Ribke to see how dramatically our health had deteriorated in such a short time, and Mum felt very self-conscious about what we must all look like.

He told Mum all about the state of our city, a story that was hard to take in. He had meant to come earlier, but the roads were so hazardous. German troops were heavily barricading themselves in, all along the road from here to Kovel. And the heavy armaments that they hauled with them were, he said, enough to blow the world up twice over. They had tried with all their might to stop the Soviets penetrating into the West, and that remained their life's mission. The Germans would fight to the death. What was in Germany's favour now was the weather. The snow was melting and their soldiers were better dressed for warmer conditions. So, it was likely to be a bloodbath that would go on for quite a while, with both sides utterly determined to kill each other.

Ribke added: 'I feel so sad bringing you such dire news; but, on the other hand, it might help you to realize that, however dreadful it is here, it is better than the situation back in town. That is just a wasteland. And, God speed, when you finally do come out of this hellish place, you will witness for yourselves all that has been inflicted upon our home.

'To my sorrow, I do not think any Jewish people are left. And I understand only too well all the strife, anger and hardship that have passed between you and my uncle. But never fear. He is a bit hot-headed, but his heart is definitely in the right place. I don't think many men would have been as compassionate in this situation. And he will make sure that you remain safe, if only for the children's sake. And I'm sure you enjoyed my aunt's *babkas*. She is the best *babka*-maker in all Ukraine and beyond. This is really the only reason I come here.'

Mum smiled.

'I'm leaving tomorrow and I will see you before I go,' he continued, then brushed himself off and gave us a sympathetic glance and shook his head in despair. The twigs were replaced and the outside world was shut away once again.

Chapter 16

'Slava'

By the end of April 1944, the memory of Mrs Yakimchuk's
babkas and the sound of cracking colourful *pysanky* had
become a distant dream, and full-blown monotony was back
on the menu, once again numbing our minds and souls. On the
positive side, Mum was beginning to get her strength back. She
was such a force of nature.

The spring days helped lift our spirits too. We couldn't see
beyond our barn but we could feel that the air had changed. It
was warmer, and smelled of spring. Outside, trees were unfurl-
ing their leaves and fields turning a hazy green with growing
crops. By the time those fields had turned golden with ripe
wheat, we would be free, Mum said. I believed it now, that this
was not going to be our life for ever, but still it was so hard
to wait.

Sometimes, to entertain herself as well as us, Mum would
wonder about the one hero we had never met, a man who held
our safety in his hands. To this day I do not know his name,
his age at the time, or anything about him, other than the

153

unkind remarks made about him by Mr Yakimchuk. I am, of course, referring to the village priest. He held such influence over the devout Mrs Yakimchuk that had he told her we must go, she might even have obeyed, however heavy her heart would have been. Such an action on his part would have been prudent, but instead he accepted the risk and kept our secret.

We would have welcomed a visit from him so that we could express our gratitude, but he never came to see us. He was very wise. In a small village like Biscobich, the appearance of the priest in the Yakimchuks' barn would have aroused much curiosity, so it was safer for everyone if he kept away.

Spring became summer. And at last in the theatre of war things were happening. Far away, in German-occupied France, the Allies launched a surprise attack, landing troops on the sandy beaches of Normandy on 6 June 1944. And a few weeks later, on 22 June, the Russians attacked the German army in Byelorussia, again taking Hitler by surprise. Reinforcements from our area were sent to help the beleaguered Germans to the north, as expected, giving the Soviet Army an opening to do what Stalin had demanded and liberate all of Ukraine.

Mr Yakimchuk, having had no real news for some time, was now coming almost daily with updates. The Germans were losing ground and it felt like the beginning of the end. We were so close; so, so close. Almost touching the rainbow.

We were convinced the Soviets would beat the hell out of the Germans. Red Army tanks were smaller and nimbler than

Nazi tanks, which were heavier than Wagnerian leading ladies. They were cumbersome and full of extra gadgets, the deployment of which was beyond the understanding of most ordinary soldiers.

And then there was the moment we had been waiting for. The Soviets were approaching Kovel in large numbers and the battle had resumed. We could hear its dark symphony of shells from miles away, piling up casualties. Such devastation.

The Germans battled on, but even the mighty roar of their Tiger tanks couldn't prevent the Soviets from finally breaking through and crushing their defences. They continued on, reaching Volodymyr-Volynskyi on 22 July 1944. A huge contingent of German fighters and their guns had stationed themselves in the city and when the battle started it was bloody, with heavy losses on both sides. It looked as if the Germans were prepared to sacrifice all they possessed in order to stop the Red Army advancing into our city and then onwards towards Berlin. Their resistance went on for quite a time. They were well dug in and evidently ready to fight to the last man.

Our city was freed at long last, and the victorious Soviets continued their march westwards. As we still remained in our refurbished state-of-the-art pit, we could hear the Red Army singing '*Kalinka kalinka kalinka moya*', and then shouting at the top of their voices to Stalin for our national 'Hurrah'. These sounds filled our souls with so much hope.

My big brother was all ready to come out. 'Mum, we are liberated. I'm off.'

'It is too early to leave,' she said, grabbing her runaway son.

The relief and excitement was beyond our wildest dreams.

Being able to go back home was all that we were praying for. The Yakimchuks came running in.

'We are free. We are liberated. Out with the Germans. A new dawn, the Soviets are here,' Mr Yakimchuk said.

The twigs were moved to one side, but they weren't taken off for good just yet. The Yakimchuks told us not to come out just yet, since Wächter's army was still on the loose. If we did, even now, it might still endanger the whole village. There was certain to be retribution if we were discovered.

We waited patiently for Ribke to come and take us back home. Two days later he arrived, filled with pride that he had helped save a mother and her three children. That was quite an accomplishment in a country at war.

We cried, we laughed, but we remained in hiding. There was a lot of congratulating and back-slapping with the Yakimchuks. 'We did it.' The old woman was full of pride and couldn't stop saying '*Slava, slava, slava.*' In all the excitement, she nearly lost her new scarf.

We were desperate to come out of our living grave, the unyielding confinement of which had so often almost made us give up hope. But Ribke was adamant: 'You must wait at least another week to ten days. It's too dangerous to take on the journey for home right now. A lot of unsavoury idiots are still about. Let the dust settle.'

We counted every minute as those ten days passed. We couldn't wait. Would we leave at night, or in the very early morning? What would we find on our return? In the end, our parting was more abrupt than we had expected. On the day we were leaving, as dawn was breaking, Mr Yakimchuk, looking demure, came to bid us farewell. He was armed with a hand-plotted map and a bombshell announcement: he would not be able to take us back home in his cart; we would have to negotiate the journey by ourselves on foot. He apologized and said he felt sickened, but told us that it was not wise for him to be seen in the company of a Jewish family. Many of the villagers would never look favourably upon them again if it became known that they had secretly kept Jews all this time and thus endangered the whole village. I wonder now why he could not have found a way to hide us in the cart but perhaps he expected to be stopped and searched. Mum, of course, unquestioningly accepted his decision with much humility. He had done so much for us that we could not ask for more.

The most pressing problem for Mum was how would her three children cope physically with the journey on foot, after nine months cooped up in the dark pit.

We left Biscobich for good, equipped with a flimsy scrap of yellowing paper – our map – together with Mr Yakimchuk's blessings and a few loaves of bread that Mrs Yakimchuk wrapped in our old tattered blanket. Although Mum was frail, and her legs barely had the strength to support her ailing body, she still held me with one hand to stop me keeling over as my own legs were now bent inwards. Lack of sunlight and space had impaired my development, causing rickets to set in. In her other hand she held the map. Haim carried on his back the blanket with the precious bread. Shalom had almost lost the ability to walk as well; he held on to a stick while attempting small frog leaps.

Our walk was shrouded in fear. We shied away from

onlookers, some of whom we believed would resent our survival and our return. Despite my mum's help, I fell over several times, possibly dislocating my arm at one point. My shoulder is still sensitive, the occasional twinges taking me back to the road from Biscobich.

The long trek seemed to stretch out to eternity and the day got hotter and hotter as the sun rose in the sky. At times we wandered off and found ourselves lost in woods; Mr Yakimchuk had many sterling qualities, but cartography was not one of them. But still we trudged on. Eventually, in the late afternoon, we reached the outskirts of Ludmir. There we stopped, and Mum took a deep breath before announcing: 'Children, we are here.'

I looked at Mum and asked with childish innocence: 'Is this Jerusalem?'

Chapter 17

Finding Home

After a long and arduous journey back home, here was our devastated town, the deeply wounded Ludmir. It stood in grief, bowing its head in shame, as if weeping for its inhabitants who had been taken away, never to return. We stopped to cast our minds back, to try to remember how it had once looked. Ours was a homecoming ensnared in anguish.

No one came to greet us; there was not one friendly face in sight to welcome us. The old neighbours shied away from us, as if we were just here to reclaim our properties, although in fact there was not a single one to be claimed. A new language dominated the place. There was no more Yiddish to be heard and now everyone spoke Russian; this was an old town robbed of its tradition. It was hard to believe this had once been the site of a thriving community, a place of business transactions, a centre for learning, a town so rich in soul and mind. What we found instead were ghosts of buildings and scattered roof tiles, once-proud chimneys leaning in sorrow, electric wires hanging from broken lampposts, as if they had had quite enough of the burden of this life. Burned books lay scattered on the ground. A few dog-eared pages survived intact, refusing to be beaten by the elements, stubbornly still telling their story. In Ludmir this was all that remained of the Reich that had been billed to last a thousand years.

It was, for all to see, a land cruelly stained by war. Tanks peppered with shell holes from the Soviet Katyusha rocket launchers lay abandoned; Panzers that had been the pride of the Wehrmacht were stained with blood and now blown to smithereens. Empty shells paved the roads. Everywhere there were Russian soldiers boasting exuberantly: '*We came to liberate you, we came to bring you peace.*'

Volodymyr-Volynskyi was now heaving with Russians, their girls parading in elaborate dresses left behind by former residents. Once, these had been worn by Jewish ladies for their Friday night blessing of the wine; nine months later, there would be a joyous *brit* (circumcision). Now, the Russians thought they were pretty party gowns. We watched as healthy, pretty girls, with plaited blonde hair, asked local bystanders where they could find a hairdresser to get a *sabithka* (perm) and, sadly, have their stunning plaits cut off.

We were trying to get to grips with this new order, to get our bearings and find where our house once stood. The Jewish cemetery – one of the oldest in Europe, going back to the fourteenth century – was quite near our house but we could barely recognize it. Headstones are sacred in Jewish culture and now we were looking at smashed stonework and gaps where they had disappeared. We later discovered that they had been used to pave the streets, walked on and probably spat on, the wanton destruction an effort to eradicate our past. Then we came across a ruin boasting a street sign, with half the letters missing. My brothers suddenly said, 'Look, Mum. This is our street.' They knew the sign so well. We were looking for our house number, but there was no number. There was no house. We stood in front of a ruin. A perfectly malign act of pointless destruction. We sat down on the bare concrete slabs that used to support our home and wept in dismay. Mum covered her face with shame. To inflict such evil upon people whose only crime had been to live here, in peace, was not natural. This was inhuman.

We had so many questions, yet so very few answers. While we were coming to terms with all this havoc inflicted by war, a Polish man stopped to speak to us. He asked, unkindly, if there were still many of us left. Mum didn't answer him, but looked at him with shocked pity. She said to us, 'Nothing has changed.'

While we sat feeling numb, a Russian lorry filled with soldiers came to a sudden halt nearby. I hid under my mother's skirt. The fear instilled in me by Hitler's soldiers had made me terrified of all men in uniforms. I became quite hysterical.

'These are our liberators. Do not fear,' Mum said, trying to pacify me.

An officer jumped off the lorry and approached us, speaking to Mum in Russian. He asked why we children looked so neglected and unkempt, and she explained. As the officer listened attentively, we could see from the way he responded that he was utterly engrossed in her story. It clearly made him so angry, and he shook his head in disbelief. Pointing to the lorry with its soldiers, he told Mum: 'We're on our way to Berlin to join General Zhukov. Luckily for you, that cruel and painful past is now over. For us, me and those young men on the truck, it's only the beginning. We're going into battle to eliminate that sadistic regime.'

They didn't know what was waiting for them in Berlin, or if they would be fortunate enough to come back. He took hold of Mum's arms to give her courage to carry on.

'You will reach a safe shore, even swimming against this tide.'

He pulled out his wallet with Russian roubles inside and handed it to Mum. 'Buy some food for your children. They could do with some. And give them a haircut. Start building a life for yourselves again'.

Mum was astonished and taken aback. Such generosity was unbelievably rare to come across in these troubled times. The soldier saw her reluctance; then he said, 'Look, where I'm going, this money is worthless. Please accept it. It will be the best act I've ever done; and it will help you until you get back on your feet. And you will.'

Mum thanked him profusely, partly of course for his generosity, but mainly for his words of encouragement, so welcome after the Pole's anti-Semitic dig.

'Maybe one day, when I come out of this hell they call war, I will look you up,' he said. But he never did. Mum kept his wallet; in it was a photograph of an old couple – his parents – and although the other contents soon vanished, the image of that officer stayed with us for ever.

Two people, so different: the ignorant Pole, and the Russian who went to war to make the world a better place.

Mum took the officer's advice. She bought some food for us and went to the water pump that stood opposite where we were sitting; we splashed ourselves with it and drank the cold nectar. For the first time I was not envious of the horse in the field. It was such a minute action and yet it was such a giant, liberating moment. We were free, and what a joy to have enough water to drink.

Although we were weary, Mum encouraged us to get going again. She needed to find somewhere for us to stay and so she took us to my grandfather's townhouse, which he would use whenever he came from the village to conduct his business. When we reached it, some strangers opened the door, clearly devastated to see us. Needless to say, they did not invite us in or offer us a glass of tea. We couldn't believe how offensive they were, especially since they had no right to occupy our family home in the first place. Mum had a long conversation with the Polish occupants. I had heard enough Polish swear words to recognize the insults of a hostile-looking man who started ranting at us. I later gathered that he was expressing his disappointment that we were still alive. He told us in no uncertain terms to leave the property and capped this 'welcome' by slamming the door so hard it nearly came off its frame. How dared we turn up and disturb his comfortable life?

After all we had been through and our exhausting journey home, this was the very last thing we needed. We stood on the doorstop while Mum thought about what to do next. Seeing us there, the lady of the house came out and said that she was going to extend a courtesy to us by allowing us to pick the cherries from the orchard that the house stood in. Our family's house, our family's orchard, our family's trees. In a climate inevitably riven with injustice, Mum was far too tired to make a fuss. 'Let it ride' was her new motto.

Eventually, Mum found a small abandoned house we could use. After the ghetto, we were used to feeling like squatters in what had once been someone else's home. I'm sure this was a sad, dusty place but it was still a luxury as far as we were concerned – a house we could move about in. A bed to sleep in. A table to eat at. Somewhere our weary, broken bodies and souls could rest and find some basic comfort at long last.

Mum went to see a miller who had been a long-standing customer of my grandfather. He was both delighted and astonished to see her. He told her that he still had some outstanding invoices which Grandad sent him before the war; but by the time they became due, Grandad was no longer with us. He truly missed Mr Akin, having conducted so many business dealings with him. The main thing that he remembered about him was what a jolly man he was, with a cracking sense of humour.

'He had to have a good sense of humour – he had six daughters,' Mum said with a smile. The miller roared with laughter.

'I tell you, you're just like your dad. When I complained to Akin about his over-charging me, he said, "What do you expect? I have to find six dowries for my daughters!"'

His advice to Mum was that it would be far better for him

to give her some flour, which was at a premium, instead of money, which had no real value now, and that she should bake bread. That would be snapped up by the hungry troops on their way to Berlin, he assured her: they were a ready-made market. Mum happily took up the miller's proposal.

At the top of Mum's agenda was to send my brothers to school. Haim and Shalom were both clever boys and Mum was keen for their education – and some semblance of normality – to resume. And Mum persuaded their headmaster to take me too, although at five I was strictly speaking too young (the usual starting age was seven). But she reasoned that I might learn something, as I missed out on so much when we were under Nazi occupation.

While we were all weakened by our incarceration, and months in a damp pit had brought on my mother's asthma, we children recovered our physical strength quite quickly. Haim and Shalom's emotional state, however, was quite a different matter: they were, understandably, consumed with anger at what had happened to us, although they usually managed to hide it. My clever brothers both did well at their lessons. Shalom came top of the school – and continued to hold that position for the rest of his school days. Haim excelled in maths and sport, just like his father. When it came it me, as there was little to be proud of I would rather not say, but I can confirm I was good at collecting the postcards depicting icons from the church. I was captivated by the vivid colours and gilding. I would exchange my pencils for the cards to Mum's fury – pencils were hard to get.

My brothers formed a group with five or six Jewish boys who had also survived the massacres, and, determined to prove they were unafraid of the bullies and the anti-Semitism that still prevailed out of school, they often got involved in fights. They would get hold of eggs and, on market days, find a strategic spot (such as the upstairs window in an empty building) from which to throw them at people who had just bought a new dress or pair of trousers. They laughed about it and felt it was retribution for what had happened to us but Mum found it dangerous rather than funny. In a bid for revenge, they even tracked down the boy who had denounced my mother to the Polish policeman, sentencing her to an almost-certain death. They beat him up very badly – Haim was just twelve and Shalom ten years of age, but children grow up very quickly in times of war and they had seen plenty of violence in their short lives. They were also badly affected when one of their group of boys committed suicide. He could no longer bear to live knowing his siblings had perished.

Meanwhile my mother was busy earning whatever she could to provide for us. I remember us getting up early in the morning to pick cherries in my grandpa's orchard so Mum could sell them. Then either she or Haim would chop wood for the outside oven, and at night she'd bake the bread with the kind miller's flour, ready to sell the following morning. She would carry big baking trays packed with rolls, three roubles each, and her bread was always quickly snapped up. When she came back from selling her stock, she'd empty her pockets of money and I would fight with my brothers to fish out the one- and three-rouble notes and count them up. I was proud of my mathematical ability, which stretched as far as knowing that thirty-three three-rouble notes, wrapped together with a one-rouble note, equalled one hundred roubles. I would stack them up neatly so Mum could use them to buy more flour for her bread.

Within a week of our arrival, Stacha, the dressmaker, came to visit, having heard that we were alive. She had fled to Poland not long after she had helped hide the boys, not wanting to live under the Russians. Now she was completely overwhelmed and ecstatic to see us again. She brought us a little box containing two bars of soap, a special comb for nits and 200 roubles. She looked so elegant in her beautiful red coat; poor Mum, in contrast, looked so impoverished, in a skirt she had made out of pyjama bottoms, and a torn blouse.

The two women sat side by side on a rickety iron bed that had to be propped up with a brick, one of its legs having been a victim of war. Mum told Stacha all about how we had come out alive, and they reminisced about how Stacha had looked after the boys and how much she had missed them. Mum spoke to Stacha in Polish but – as I had lived the story – I felt I understood the gist of what she was telling her, if not every word. I certainly recognized the name Yakimchuk that was constantly mentioned.

Within a short time, Mum's money-making efforts had begun to pay off. I was resplendent in a new pair of shoes made of crocodile leather, which was all she could get hold of.

Leather was at a premium, as most of the tanneries had been emptied by the Germans – they were obscenely obsessed with leather. She made me a pinafore out of some old blackout lining. I was so proud of my new look. It was very 1940s, bang on trend. My couture surely inspired Christian Dior for the Paris Fashion Week.

Once we had a roof over our heads, the Yakimchuks often came to visit. Mum was very house-proud, and everything was so sparkly and nice that the Yakimchuks would refuse to come into the house. The boys had to literally carry them inside, so anxious were they not to create any sort of mess. They couldn't believe how quickly we had established ourselves.

In our city, only about thirty adults and nine children had survived, out of 25,000 Jews. Two of these, Dr Levit and his wife, also came to see us. They had been sheltered by two brave Polish families, first in the countryside where they had a hiding place under the straw in a threshing pen during the winter of 1942 to 1943, and then in Ludmir itself where the parents of a nurse Dr Levit had worked with hid them in a cellar. Whenever I took Mum to see him in Israel after the war, there would be a Polish lady with him who was one of those who had saved him. She didn't want to stay in the city after the war and so Dr Levit brought her to Israel and cared for her for the rest of her life. What a lovely end to a sad story.

Mum immediately told the doctor about Paraska, the Yakimchuks' daughter who remained seriously ill. He suggested they bring her to see him at once. He determined that Paraska urgently needed to be X-rayed to find out more about her condition, but such a machine was no longer available in

Volodymyr-Volinskyi. The Germans had ransacked all the hospitals.

There were so few Jews left in Ukraine that news quickly spread about who had survived, and Mum heard about a female Jewish doctor in Lutsk, a city around seventy-five kilometres to the east, who did have X-ray equipment. When she got to her clinic with the Yakimchuks she found it was packed with people waiting to be X-rayed but the doctor didn't have any oil to get the machine going. My determined mother stood in the middle of the road and flagged down a Russian army lorry on its way to the front, begging for a can of oil. The driver was furious.

'Listen, woman, what the hell are you playing at? We are on our way to Berlin and you have the audacity to hold us up.'

Mum apologized profusely and gave him a bottle of vodka and a packet of Machaka (Russian tobacco). The driver was delighted with this deal and Mum got the oil.

Dr Levit was such a wonderful help to us, and he had such a lot of time for Mum. While he was treating the ailing Paraska, Mum also asked him to look at my painful arm, which had come out of its socket when I fell over on our way back to Volodymyr-Volynskyi from Biscobich. He put it in a sling and it soon got better.

It took quite a while before Paraska saw any improvement, but with some expensive medicine and plenty of care, Dr Levit did manage to get her back on her feet again, and she was able to return home. I never found out exactly what was wrong with her, but Mum believed that if Dr Levit had attended her at least three years earlier, he might have been able to cure her completely. Paraska seemed quite well after the war, and was perhaps eager to make up for the time she had lost to illness. One day she insisted on going out in bad weather with her friends and caught a bad cold that went to her lungs. Alas, with no doctor in Biscobich and no medication she faded away. Her death left a big void in the Yakimchuk family.

Chapter 18

Refugees

We remained in Volodymyr-Volynskyi – the Jewish name of Ludmir seemed no longer appropriate – for another eighteen months, during which time my mother recovered some of her old strength, or seemed to, outwardly, at least. We had no choice but to get on with life in our shattered little city, and gradually schools, shops and even the cinema – where I remember seeing a Charlie Chaplin film – reopened for those who remained. My ever-resourceful mother managed to make good money by going to Poland to buy products that weren't available in Ukraine and selling them for an excellent return. She took Haim with her to buy caustic soda in bulk, needing his strength to carry it home. After school, he would uncomplainingly help her cut it up into smaller blocks to sell on, both their eyes reddened and sore from the tiny specks that flew into the air. She also bought yeast in bulk, again cutting it into smaller pieces, and went to Kiev to buy mountains of exercise books and pencils, which would arrive by the lorryload. She always thought big, saying, 'Stock is king in bad times. If you buy small amounts, you put in exactly the same time and effort, and the return is pitiful, especially when you trade in low value items.'

While Mum was busy trying to make enough to keep us fed and clothed, she also had to be careful that her 'capitalist' activities did not bring her to the notice of our new authorities. We were once again part of a communist totalitarian state that flung into prison anyone considered enemies of the revolution. It is one of the reasons why Mum did nothing when Zavidovich, the head of the Jewish police, arrived back in the city. He had somehow managed to escape death when the third ghetto was destroyed and, with so few survivors left, he no doubt hoped to avoid retribution too. Mum didn't want to report him and find herself under scrutiny. In addition, Mum knew she had only enough strength for the three key tasks she had set herself: to earn a living, to make sure the Yakimchuks were taken care of, and to ensure Ribke was safe.

Not long after we'd arrived Mum went to see Ribke to thank him for finding us a safe place during those darkest days of our lives. He was so brave. But alas this was a time of reprisals and payback, and Ribke was soon in deep trouble. The Russians were after him and, if they caught up with him, he could expect at best to be sent to a Gulag in Siberia, and at worst to be executed.

Mum was always practical in times of adversity (she had a lot of experience to draw from). She packed her satchel – that bag could tell its own story, it had a very chequered life – and headed off to the offices of the commissariat with her three children in tow as key witnesses for the defence.

She told the receptionist, in her fluent Russian, that she had an appointment with the commissar in charge. It was untrue, but she was clearly a woman who would not be easily fobbed off and that at least got her into the building. Mum went to the nearest desk to ask if she could see the man who was in charge of the new assembly. She lacked the patience to deal with junior staff on serious matters; she always went straight to the top. And while she was talking, a group of men came past.

'Mrs Fischmann, you are alive!' one of them exclaimed. 'And the three children! I am stunned. And your husband?'

Mum just looked down, and the answer must have been obvious.

We were taken to the man's office. I cannot remember his name, though I assume he was an important member of the new regime. I do remember us sitting round a table that was over-flowing with papers rubber-stamped in violet ink. I was very familiar with this ink, which always managed to adorn my new pinafore and crocodile shoes. Mum would chide me for not being more careful, but it was never my fault, as I always pointed out.

'I just can't believe this,' he said again. 'You are here. Alive.'

He was the political prisoner who had thrown us bread and garlic out of the window of his cell as he was waiting to see what his fate would be, just before the German officer and my uncle rescued us from death.

'It was an unforgettable picture,' he said. 'I watched the three small children trying to break the bread with frozen hands. And then you were being pushed towards the death column. And not one of those thousands of people came out alive. Except you!'

Mum was a little enthralled by him – he was actually happy

to see us and determined to hear our story, unlike so many of the people we encountered in the city. Now he wanted to know how we had managed to survive. It gave Mum the perfect opportunity to mention Ribke and his part in saving us.

Just before we were about to leave, the man suddenly excused himself and went out for a couple of minutes. Mum took the opportunity to surreptitiously put two bottles of French cognac under the desk, a thank you and perhaps a down-payment on his future goodwill. And when he returned, under his arm he was carrying a black loaf of bread with the number '68' written on it in white chalk. The numbered loaf was part of the benevolent largesse that was being dispensed by Stalin. And every week, from that time onwards, we went over to the office to collect our Russian bread.

The cognac came from the swag that the Germans, in their frantic hurry to get away, had had to leave behind. Mum knew people in the city and must have traded for it.

Mum also went to court to give evidence on Ribke's behalf, saying what a wonderful human being he was. It was a typical Soviet court after the war, when connections and cash could have bought up half of Ukraine. Although Mum never explicitly said so, I'm assuming that money was the best defence, and Mum saw to it that Ribke became a free man once again. With a huge sigh of relief.

Although Mum was busy and purposeful, earning a living and creating a home for her children, she was a woman still grieving the loss of her husband, her parents, and almost all the rest of her family. There was no longer a community to support her. She did not want to remain in what had been our home city. After the defeat of Germany in May 1945, travel became more of a possibility, and Mum put her mind to earning enough money to fund our get away.

The Yakimchuks came to see us and say their farewells. Mrs Yakimchuk was finding it very hard to leave, overcome with emotional memories of our life in Biscobich, rubbing her face in her warm old wrap. The old man wept when he parted from Haim. It was all so hard. No mash, no baked potatoes; just vivid, painful memories of war.

We had all been through so much together and emerged alive. The price for our salvation was beyond anything we could ever repay. We waved them off as their cart, which was boasting new wheels with steel trimmings, set off on the road back to Biscobich.

And in case you wondered, Mr Yakimchuk never exchanged his old horse for a newer model, even though, as the owner of a large farm, he could have afforded a whole cavalry. There's loyalty.

A few days later, on a warm mid summer's day in 1946, we left Volodymyr-Volynskyi, although Ludmir would remain in our hearts for the rest of our days. My mother had prepared well for the journey, which included visiting the cobbler who had made our family's shoes for many years. She asked him to create two soles for hers and my brothers' shoes, between which they could conceal a layer of gold sovereigns. She also carried with her a little barrel-shaped vessel full of lard, which she pretended she needed to feed us children, but which also contained gold sovereigns. She didn't, of course, trust me with any sovereigns, although I remember a few flew out of one of my brother's shoes when he played football one day, and we were left scrabbling to retrieve them.

With my family now literally walking on gold, the next stop of our odyssey was Lviv, where we stayed for a few weeks while she arranged for us to leave the country. Mum rented a flat opposite the opera house and I mostly remember being captivated by the trams that rattled through the square below our window. Then it was on to Bytom, Poland, where we might perhaps have settled for a while had it not soon become apparent that although the Nazis were defeated, the torch of anti-Semitism was kept burning strongly by the surviving natives. On 4 July 1946 there was a pogrom in Kielce in which forty-two Jews, all survivors of the Holocaust, were murdered by an angry Polish mob. Why were they so angry? Hadn't they had their fill of killing yet? It convinced Mum that it was time for us to move on. This and other violent pogroms in Poland caused many like us – an estimated 100,000 people in fact – to leave the country and head west to territories liberated by the Allies.

My abiding memory of our train journey out of Poland was Mum's strict instruction to the three of us not to speak Yiddish. We knew that round here Jews got thrown off moving trains. We rode in silence to Katowice and then on to the Czech border. There, as we walked past the frontier guard post, a Polish soldier tried to grab Mum's fur coat from her back. Mum protested, 'No, this is my coat', but the guard reached for his gun. Then a Czech guard in the nearby sentry box on the other side of the frontier intervened, telling the Pole that he had better let Mum go. Reluctantly, he did. When we had safely entered Czechoslovakia, the same guard told us, 'Look, you are free now. We are not like the Poles, we are a nation apart.'

Perhaps he was right, but we didn't stay in his country for long. As refugees we were scheduled to be transferred directly to Vienna. As we waited for hours on the outskirts of Bratislava for a car to take us into Austria, Haim got bored and wandered off into the nearby woods, he said to pick berries. When the car eventually arrived, there was no sign of Haim. Mum was immediately alarmed, but the forest rangers told her not to worry, reminding her 'You're not in Poland now.' Eventually someone said they'd seen a little boy on his own standing by a well. Naturally, in view of our experiences in wartime Ukraine, this really made Mum panic, but again the rangers reassured her. They hurried off and after some time finally returned with my bleary-eyed brother, who had fallen asleep on the woodland floor.

From Vienna we were sent to a displaced persons' camp in the American-occupied zone of Salzburg. This was perhaps the worst part of our post-war experience as the conditions there were dreadful. The place was filled with broken Jewish souls who had somehow survived the ghettos and concentration camps. And while we might have escaped the violence of Poland or our homelands, we sensed the locals were not happy to have Jews in their midst. Without the Jews, they seemed to think, Hitler would have been victorious.

My recollections of our dismal life in Salzburg are stronger, perhaps because I was a little older now at seven years old. I was aware that we were living in cramped conditions, largely in huts. Food was scarce, and what little there was of it was inedible. In the morning we would queue with a basin for our daily portion of soup, often just some boiled water with potatoes, and I would count myself lucky if a whole potato plopped into my bowl, a dish that I think most pigs would have turned their snouts away from. I had few, if any, friends in that camp, simply because there were very few children there, so many having been murdered. Children in Eastern Europe were particularly vulnerable under the Nazi regime, starved to death in the ghettos or among the first to be killed in the mass shootings or gas chambers. It brought home to us that our survival was truly miraculous.

We endured another eight months in Salzburg, during which time scouts from the underground organization Bricha (Hebrew for 'flight' or 'escape') came to prepare us for resettlement in Palestine. After all we had been through, a Jewish homeland in Palestine, the future state of Israel, seemed to offer the only safe haven; a place where we could build a new life and find true sanctuary.

To get to Palestine, however, we needed to make our way to Italy, travelling along an illegal route facilitated by Bricha to the south of the country. We were keen to leave Austria as fast possible, but because the journey involved an arduous night trek over the Alps, along paths deep in snow, the scouts were happy to take my mother and brothers but not me. Yet again my young age caused problems for my family, but my brothers assured the scouts that they would take responsibility for me and persuaded them to let me go.

The trek over the Alps took place at night, in the pitch black, and was indeed steep and exhausting. There was a long trail of around 120 people, all strangers, and the snow was deep. But my brothers helped me through the thickest of the drifts, sometimes carrying me on their backs – that was their reward for having a younger sister, poor boys.

I later learned that senior Nazis – the *capos* of the concentration camps and rulers of the ghettos – were hiding in the Alps, trying to escape justice by the Allies, and that they took the same route as us from Innsbruck to Milan and thence to Rome. The Holy See was issuing false passports for them to escape to South America, taking stolen wealth from Europe with them. So perhaps along the way we walked with Josef Mengele and Adolf Eichmann, and maybe Otto Wächter.

When we came to the Italian border – the authorities there turning a blind eye to the arrival of refugees – we were boarded onto a truck. People threw oranges for us to eat – I'd never had one before. I remember so well the tangy sweetness of that first bite, its bright, sunny colour seeming to represent everything that Italy had to offer. Everything about the place felt instantly different – the people, the landscape and culture. To us, Italy was a symphony of joy.

The truck rumbled on for several hours, eventually dropping us off at a displaced persons' camp in Rome. The name 'Cinecittà' ('cinema city') was emblazoned on its entrance, as the buildings had once contained film studios, the largest in Europe. Cinecittà had been established during the fascist regime of Mussolini, was bombed by the Allies during the war, then converted into a refugee camp. We were housed with other refugees in a large hangar-like studio, its walls padded with insulation, I presume to keep noise out during filming. By then, I'd had some exposure to movies, of course, and the Charlie Chaplin films we had watched in Volodymyr-Volynskyi provided us with welcome escapism in those months after our incarceration ended, but it's strange to think that – not long after we left as refugees – the film studios opened up again and welcomed Hollywood stars through the doors for productions as famous as *Cleopatra* and *Ben-Hur*.

While conditions at Cinecittà were fairly basic and we slept on little more than camp beds, life felt more hopeful: the Italians seemed so much friendlier and more welcoming than the Austrians, and of course the camp had the added benefit of Mediterranean sunshine.

After a few days, we were taken to a camp in Milan, this time an army barracks quite close to the Pirelli factory. There were far more children there, many of whom had come from Russia where the young had had a much greater chance of survival than in Eastern Europe. For the first time in my life I could make friends – we were all broken in some way and had been through the same experiences, but we didn't dwell on them. My best friend Gita, who had travelled from Russia, had also lost her father who had perished in a Gulag. She had the most beautiful mass of black curly hair which she would twist into ringlets. I was just the opposite with my straight blonde locks. The thing I most liked about her was that she was jolly when I was sad – she was very good for me. Gita's brother Zwoolen was Haim's best friend. Another girl, Dorca, tried to befriend us, but we would never let her get too close. Looking back, I think it was because she had both her parents and Gita and I were a little jealous.

I was now old enough to attend the schools set up by the Palestine scouts, where we learned Hebrew and my brothers could play football. Shalom was the teachers' and headmaster's dream pupil, much to my annoyance. As usual I was just the sister of the clever brother. We three children were also sent away on holidays, designed to help with our recuperation and to build our strength for our eventual emigration to Palestine. I remember staying for a month in Lake Como with the school, during which time I was a little ill with a sore throat – I always seemed to come down with something during holidays. My mother came – not once, but twice – to see us there, the only mother I remember doing so – she clearly still felt anxious about our welfare. Mind you, she liked to travel, so perhaps this was also her chance to see Como.

While we were in Italy, Mum was able to keep a promise that years before she had pledged to Uncle Morris's mother, my mum's grandmother. She too had been sent to the first ghetto, and her rift with her son played on her mind constantly. Although she was unable to read or write, she wanted to dictate a letter to Morris, forgiving him for abandoning his faith and renewing her loving bond.

She had an idea that, of all her relatives, my mum was the one with the best chance of surviving the war, so she asked her to write it all down and hold on to the letter for safe keeping. My great-grandmother was shot during the first pogrom.

As I wrote earlier, when Mum got her blue pass to work in

the second ghetto, she made a linen bag to hang around her neck, in which she kept her 'permit to live'. And throughout the remainder of our ordeal, she kept Morris's mother's letter safely alongside it.

When we made it to Italy, our names were posted there as survivors, and the list was eventually seen by Morris, who contacted us. And, by this means, Mum was able to send Morris that sacred letter from his mother, a message that would have meant so much to him, the words telling of a mother's love and forgiveness. During the first few years in Israel, we continued to correspond with Morris, who wrote in Yiddish to Mum and in Hebrew to me, although he sadly died of a sudden heart attack before he was able to visit us. Not being able to meet him was a tragedy for me. He inspired me to write essays and to paint with words the sights I saw. In one of his letters to me he wrote that my description of Mount Carmel made him long to walk among the bright red poppies and pale pink crocuses that carpeted the peak.

We stayed a year in Milan and then travelled south to a camp in Trani in Puglia, forty kilometres west of Bari. It was a small coastal town and it felt like we were on a seaside holiday. I remember swimming in the warm Adriatic Sea and also catching measles, a common infection in those pre-vaccine days, from which I quickly recovered.

Just up the coastline from Trani lay the port of Bari, where we were due to board a ship that would take us to a new life in the fledgling state of Israel. The country had officially come into being earlier that year, on 14 May 1948. After a year and a half in Italy, the day of our sailing finally came. Our allotted ship, an aged Greek vessel named *Teti*, had clearly seen better days – it had more holes than a string vest – but, somehow, it survived the choppy waters of the Adriatic and Mediterranean seas, which can at times get quite rough.

Our first time on a ship was an adventure for us children, but the rocking motion made poor Mum very ill with seasickness – and she wasn't alone. A large number of passengers had been crammed on board, including many refugees from North Africa, which marked the first time we had encountered Jewish people who looked different and had customs that were very different to us. All we had in common was our faith. It was also a ship packed with emotion – some passengers couldn't wait to begin a new life in the Promised Land, and were excited to be some of the first legal immigrants to arrive in Israel. My mother, on the other hand, had mixed feelings about going to Israel and worried that we had escaped one war only to head into another, as Jews were fighting Arabs in Palestine in the ongoing War of Independence. She would have happily gone to America or England, but my brothers and I had learned Hebrew at school and we had our hearts set on going to the Jewish homeland with all our friends. We arrived in Haifa on 20 November 1948, a date for ever etched in my memory. We children felt nothing but happy anticipation as Mount Carmel came into view.

Chapter 19

The Promised Land

It was pouring with rain and very cold in Haifa. We were old hands now at the process of arriving in a new country, queuing, being moved around by officials. It felt different this time, though. We had finally arrived at our destined land.

We were first put up in the transit camp of Binyamina just outside Tel Aviv. Amid the rain and mud, we slept in tents, and at night we could hear hyenas screaming – it really was dreadful. Not unsurprisingly, my mother decided we weren't going to put up with these conditions for longer than a couple of nights, and she demanded to be transferred to a town. Through her sheer persistence, we were moved to a different camp in Haifa, a home for immigrants, and on to a modest house in the town with a simple corrugated-iron roof on the kitchen, which always leaked when it rained, and which had two Primus stoves for cooking. In those early years in Israel, people made do with relatively little, and we had least of all.

We then moved to another little house just outside Tel Aviv, which became our family home. Mum put all her efforts into building a life for us. She didn't work, partly because she had enough money to get by; she had a few sovereigns left over from Volodymyr-Volinskyi, and in subsequent years reparation payments from Germany for Holocaust victims and a pension kept her solvent. But, in truth, the war had left her badly damaged – she had very bad asthma and suffered from frequent headaches, largely due to the blow to the head she had received from the Polish policeman. She had been spared a bullet through the head, of course, but a small dent in her skull bore permanent testament to one man's violent hatred.

At the same time my mother was very good at hiding her suffering, partly helped by swallowing painkillers for the rest of her life, which eased her discomfort. It also wasn't my mother's way to talk about how she felt; perhaps that was to protect us, knowing how much we had all been through and not wanting to burden us further. As a family, we talked, but not about her deep feelings, and I knew not to raise such matters with Mum. Children don't have the words to articulate what they know instinctively, and I understood that she was a tormented woman.

At times, Mum was frustrated by life in Israel where, as she feared, war was still a looming presence. She still wondered whether America might have been a better choice. She would occasionally go to the synagogue. Having been brought up in a Chassidic home, she knew her Bible very well, and had been shaped by the rituals of Judaism in her early years. And yet, having witnessed such atrocities and seen the evil humans could do to each other, she had mostly lost her faith.

*

By the time we were settled in Israel, I was nearly ten years old and my brothers were already teenagers – Shalom was fifteen and Haim almost a grown man at seventeen. So much of their childhoods had been taken up with war, day-to-day survival and life as refugees, and now they stood on the cusp of adulthood. They were both bright, academic boys and did well at school, after which they were conscripted into the Israeli army. Thereafter Haim briefly studied engineering in France and the US before pursuing a career in that field, principally working for the military. He later married and has two fine sons. Shalom also married, towards the tail-end of his army years, and he ended up working in electronics. He has two beautiful daughters. Both my brothers are still living in Israel.

Despite their blighted childhoods, they got on with their lives, although that's not to say they weren't impacted by the Holocaust. We all cope in different ways, and Shalom, who saw with his own eyes so much horror, prefers not to speak of his experiences and never wants to dwell on it. Of course none of us did dwell on it, but Haim and I could talk a little more about what happened.

For me, the trauma manifested in unexpected ways. Strangely, I suffered more nightmares as an adult than when I was a child, and during the night my husband David would hear me shout out for my mother as my subconscious relived the horrors of the past. But growing up, I was something of a sad, pensive child; people remarked that I didn't often have a smile on my face. I never talked about that sadness, although it might sometimes come out in my writing and essays at school.

Added to this, during the first few years in Israel I felt like an outsider, partly because the survivors from the war and newer immigrants were often looked down upon by those who had settled in the country earlier. We were viewed by some as weak and submissive – why didn't we fight back? – and at school there was little mixing between the Israeli girls and the survivors, which angered me then. In my opinion they were right to say that we should have retaliated and killed a few Germans, Poles and Ukrainians. But the situation was complex and the Nazis were very methodical. At first they killed all the young men, the ones who could have fought. They created discord between the Poles and Ukrainians, so both were happy to kill Jews. The Poles were anti-Semites who hated the Jews, and the Ukrainians wanted the spoils. By the time Reinhard Heydrich came up with the Final Solution, we were done. But the old settlers did not have to rub in that we were damaged goods. A bit of tolerance and compassion would have gone a long way.

On the whole, however, I enjoyed school and made some good friends, in particular Esther Goldman, who also came from Ludmir, and with her sister and mother had survived the Holocaust. They went to live in a kibbutz, and I spent many wonderful holidays with them.

While we might not have delved deep into our innermost feelings as a family, our conversations were invariably peppered with references to the past as we chatted over dinner, with the delicious aroma of cholent wafting in from the kitchen. Mum delighted in cooking for us, and she always had plenty of food in, especially when my brothers were home on leave from the army. As she herself said: 'I always buy twice as much as I need. I'm trying to compensate you three for all the years you went without.'

On such family get-togethers, Mum would often take out her precious Rosenthal plates with gilded edges – porcelain that was once much coveted in Europe and made her think nostalgically of Ludmir. Sometimes I would joke with Mum that I'd happily eat anything so long as it wasn't lumpy mash, to which she'd invariably answer, 'Now listen, don't be so dismissive of Mrs Y's mash. If it wasn't for her, you wouldn't be having blintzes [pancakes] today! Her mash kept us going for the best part of a year against all the odds.'

Whenever the boys came to Mum's house, she took on a new lease of life; but then, when they went, her mood changed, becoming somewhat melancholic. Of the three of us children, she was most attached to Shalom – he was admittedly very handsome and clever, and was affected by the war slightly more than Haim and myself. But there is rarely any logic to the dynamics of families. It was my big brother Haim who understood my mother best and cared for her the most.

When the four of us got together, we shared a similar sense of humour that only we found funny. It was always connected to our shenanigans with the Yakimchuks.

On one occasion over dinner, my Rosenthal plate predictably overflowing so much that I could no longer see its garish gilded borders, we were eating blintzes which were accompanied by some cherry liqueur that Shalom had brought. Fancying himself as a bit of a connoisseur, he had made it himself, supplying it in shapely bottles with rather creative labels.

I took out my glasses to see what vintage his latest creation was. Regrettably my mouth was full so that when I burst out with an uncontrollable laugh, Mum's beautifully pressed white linen tablecloth fell victim to my blintz explosion. I couldn't stop howling. Mum asked what was so funny and it was only after I had read out the label of Shalom's cherry liqueur, 'Chateau Le Pit 1944', that she too joined in the laughter.

As soon as I could speak, I apologized profusely.

'Don't be silly,' she said. 'I love it when you can laugh out loud, after so long suppressing your emotions. I always had to say, "Shush, the Germans will find us," and put my hand over your mouth to keep you quiet.'

And she was right, I had a tendency to bottle up my emotions, was never much of an attention-seeker and was always much happier in the background. Even today, when I am overcome with laughter, I find myself feeling guilty, thinking maybe I shouldn't be showing my feelings after all.

Chapter 20

A New Beginning

At the age of twenty, in 1959, I decided to have a small adventure. By then I had a good job working as a PA for a large national company, but I wanted to take a few weeks off to travel around Europe, and my employers were happy to keep my role open for my return. It was quite unusual for the times, for a young woman to go travelling, but I was keen to see the world and to experience how others lived. The trip would prove life-changing in a way I could not have foreseen.

My good friend Aviva came with me and we flew first to Greece, where I particularly delighted in Athens, and from there we headed to Italy by boat and took in the beauty of Naples, Venice and Rome. Of course, I had a fondness for the country that so many years before had provided a sanctuary for me and my family. I remembered how that warm Mediterranean light had provided a balm for our shattered souls, and I still had a smattering of Italian. Sitting in the Piazza San Marco in Venice, sipping coffee with Aviva, I found myself thinking about how much water had flowed under the Rialto Bridge since I had last been in the country.

From Italy, we travelled to Geneva, where we visited the United Nations, located in the impressive Art Deco Palais des Nations overlooking Lake Geneva. As awe-inspiring as the building was, I was particularly taken by two huge paintings in the lobby, by the Brazilian artist Candido Portinari. They depicted a wartime scene, with two mothers holding their children, one of whom was protecting her child with her hair. I stood and took in the poignancy of that image, a child whose mother had fought like a lion for her survival, and sixty-odd years later I still remember that painting with such clarity and emotional affiliation.

Aviva and I then travelled on to Paris, where we visited the usual sights and caught the attention of some handsome Yugoslav footballers who were staying at our hotel. We were astonished that wherever we went in Paris, they seemed to magically appear, until it dawned on us that they had overheard our conversations with the hotel front desk. We were flattered by the attention, and I felt very cheerful in Paris, so much so that, while wandering around the grounds of Sacré-Coeur, I agreed to have my portrait painted as a memento of the trip. After studying my face, the artist commented: 'You know, you look very sad,' and he proceeded to paint me with a pensive expression, despite my happy mood that day!

After France, we spent some time in San Sebastián and Madrid in Spain, and from there flew to London where Aviva had an uncle. I stayed for a couple of days, walking the streets of London in awe as I took in the architecture, before I headed north to Newcastle. There I visited the children of Grandma Miriam's sister, Manny and Morris and their sister Elsie. I was surprised by how little knowledge they had about the Holocaust and by what seemed like their lack of interest, but perhaps they did not want to upset me by asking questions.

After a few days I went to the Lincolnshire fishing port of Grimsby, where Elsie lived with her family. Huge trawlers filled the docks and the town seemed to be very prosperous, a place where money could be made.

On the second or third day a guy appeared, a friend of Elsie's son called David. He was wearing Bata suede safari boots, and looked like a white hunter, but the attire made sense when I discovered he was a journalist and was helping to set up the *Daily Nation* newspaper in Nairobi. Not long before our trip I'd watched *Love Is a Many-Splendored Thing* and had jokingly announced to Aviva that I was going to marry a foreign correspondent. Now, here I was, actually meeting one! About six months after I'd returned home, David came to Israel for work and looked me up. We enjoyed each other's company but I was still very surprised when I went to say goodbye to him at the airport and he informed me that in six months' time I would be in Kenya with him!

The next thing I knew I received a cable from BOAC to say that there was a plane ticket to Nairobi waiting for me – and I made the decision to go. While I was excited to be living abroad, it was of course hard to leave my family, although I think Mum was happy for me to follow my heart and to move on with my life. David and I married and we lived in Nairobi for the next seven years, during which time I had two children – a son Avi and a daughter Elaine. Kenya made for a great start in married life, but we never planned to live there for ever, and in 1972 we made the decision to move to England, where David could better pursue his journalistic career.

We lived first in Newark and then West Bridgford in Nottinghamshire and I was very happy to be in England. I felt contented in a way I never quite had before, and the reserved, rather phlegmatic nature of the British appealed to me. In Israel, you tell a story and everyone reacts as if it's something huge, whereas the Brits are less given to emotion, and I like that, perhaps because it chimes with my own character. The British sense of humour also appeals to me – no one does irony quite like the Brits, except perhaps my mother.

For all that I was happy in England, I never sought to forget the trauma of my younger years and was always keen to keep in contact with the few surviving members of my extended family, particularly those who knew my mother and father. My memories of our time in the ghetto and captivity were blurred – my mother told us what she could, but I sensed she held back on so many of the details. As for my dad, I knew so little about him that I always yearned for someone to fill in the blanks. On one of my visits to Israel I had tried to get Mum to talk about him, nerving myself to broach what I knew would be a difficult subject.

'Mum, can I ask you about Dad? I'd love to hear more about him, and what he was like. I don't remember him at all.'

'Of course,' Mum said. 'Let's have a cup of tea and we can be comfortable and talk.'

She busied herself boiling water for the tea and slicing lemon while I marshalled my thoughts. We had just sat down together when Mum suddenly jumped up and said, 'Malka, I am so sorry but I forgot my hair appointment. I have to hurry or I'll be late.'

She rushed to put on her coat and pick up her handbag. It was only as the door closed behind her that I remembered she always had her hair done on a Friday, and today was Thursday.

I didn't have the heart to try again, but I did get the chance to learn more in the 1980s when Mum rang to tell me that our cousin Rachel, who now lived in the United States, was coming to England. The last time I had seen Rachel was when I was four years old, after she, with Ribke, had helped secure our survival during the war. She had stayed in touch, even sending us food parcels from her displaced persons camp in Germany when we first arrived in Israel, where food was rationed. One of her packages included a stylish little handbag for me, making me the envy of all my friends. Now I was thrilled to have the chance to see her again and I hoped she could shed more light on those crucial years in Ludmir.

After the war, she had emigrated to the US, where she remarried and went on to have twin girls, Rose and Pearl. I asked Mum what she looked like now so that I'd know who I was collecting from the airport. She assured me that Rachel would recognize me – I assume she'd seen photographs – and that she was a tall, coquettish lady who didn't 'look particularly Jewish', reminding me that during the war she had managed to obtain Aryan papers as a result of her looks.

The night before her arrival couldn't pass fast enough. In the morning, I went to collect Rachel from Heathrow, and it took no time at all for us to fall into each other's arms. It was a cold November day and it was raining heavily. Welcome to England, Rachel!

We instantly began reminiscing in the car and the journey passed quickly. The rain had stopped by the time we arrived at my home in Nottinghamshire. I unlocked the door and beckoned her in, urging her to treat my house as her own. Inside, we fell into each other's arms again and wept.

'Ludmir feels light years away,' Rachel said.

By now, it was late in the afternoon, and Rachel went upstairs to unpack. I lit a fire and set a table for two for tea.

When she came down, the two of us sat down to drink some tea, Rachel politely choosing to drink it with milk and in a cup, rather than in a glass with a little lemon, which is the Russian way and how my mother preferred it. I suggested she help herself to the milk jug, but she changed her mind.

'Would it be rude if I asked for a slice of lemon?'

'Rachel, for you, a whole grove would not be enough,' I replied. 'We owe our lives to you. You're the one who found Ribke. You put yourself in grave danger when you went to see Ribke to persuade him to find us a safe house during the war.'

Rachel couldn't hold back her tears. 'You don't know the

whole story. It was your mother who hatched the whole plan. I was just delivering the message.'

'Oh please, Rachel, I can't wait to hear about it. It's so difficult to pin Mum down when it comes to Ribke's saga and the story of my father. Why is it so difficult for Mum to open up?'

'Your mum's never been good at sharing her feelings with others, but she has always kept your dad's memory deep in her soul. Her heart has been broken beyond mending. You can't put sticking plaster on a broken heart; the pain is always there.'

'Yes, that's so true, Rachel. But I'm a bit surprised that Mum was so shattered; she always appeared so strong.'

'Don't be fooled. She was putting on a brave face for you lot.'

'Losing Dad was so very hard for us all. I used to be so envious of girls who had fathers as a child, when I was growing up. How different my life would have been.'

The following day, I took Rachel on a scenic trip to Derbyshire. It was a magnificent autumn day and the sun was shining in all its glory. I longed for Rachel to soak up a bit of the green and pleasant land.

I drove through the Chatsworth estate along the banks of the splendid River Derwent. Rachel wanted to take some photos so she could take some back to her adopted country. I stopped the car. 'Are you ready for a walk, Rach?'

'How can I say no? I'm in awe of that magnificent stately home.'

'Yes, but Debo the duchess who lives here had tea with Hitler! One of her sisters was so obsessed with Hitler that she shot herself when war was declared. And the husband of one of the others was the leader of a fascist party in England. He was jailed for organizing anti-Semitic rallies. There were definitely some British aristocrats who admired the Nazis, like the king, Edward VIII.'

The two of us walked along the river, crushing the autumn leaves beneath our feet. As I watched the gentle ripple of the waters of the River Derwent, my mind drifted back to the ghetto, when we were effectively imprisoned and I could only watch bathers and strollers along the banks of the River Luha through the small window of our little house. The contrast could hardly have been greater.

'You know, Rachel, autumn is my favourite time of year. It's as though you are putting a season of hustle and bustle to rest. One day, I would love to spend autumn in Vermont. You call it "fall" over there: such a lovely description. It's painted in my mind. I can just see the leaves falling from the sycamores.'

'It seems to me you're a bit of a romantic dreamer,' Rachel told me.

'Not so sure about romantic, but certainly a dreamer. I had to be, as my world was so dark for so long. I had no childhood. Most girls dream of dolls and beautiful dresses. My dream was to be lucky enough to get a potato dropped in murky water.'

We had a long, brisk walk around Baslow, the nearest village to Chatsworth. As we drank in the beauty of the landscape, our boots covered in mud and oak leaves, I explained to Rachel that I was keen to understand what kind of man Dad was, and that throughout my life, I had always tried to embroider an ideal picture of him. He seemed like a man in a hurry to me. But obviously, the picture I was building was probably not a bit like who he really was.

'Your dad wasn't your typical early twentieth-century shtetel man. He had a talent for languages, his main interests were sport and mechanics; that's why he started a bicycle shop. The shop was quite a sizeable, buzzing business. It was a meeting-point for enthusiasts, who exchanged bikes for the latest models and all the latest must-have gadgets. Your dad loved all that part of it much more than the business side. That's where your clever mum came in. She was always thinking about the next deal.'

I asked Rachel about Ribke and how well she or my parents knew him. He was among the very few who were prepared to put their heads on the block for us, so I had assumed there must have been some connection I didn't know about.

'No, I hardly knew the guy,' explained Rachel. 'The first time I appeared on his doorstep was after your mum first mentioned him. My part was just to liaise between your mum and him. He did, however, have a connection with your dad.'

I discovered that Ribke had been a regular at my dad's bicycle shop. He was forever having altercations with his machine and, at times, he would come in with his wheel turned into a figure of eight or with the dynamo coming away from the frame. While the men in Dad's workshop were busy putting Ribke's bicycle back together, he would talk to my dad and the two got to know each other a little.

'Once, when Ribke was back yet again, your dad said, "I hope it's not a problem with the bike I sold you." And Ribke said, "No, it's a problem with the road to Biscobich!"

'That's how your dad found out that Ribke had an aunt and uncle in Biscobich. He spoke a lot about them and was obviously very close to them. Your dad had told your mum this and planted the idea that Ribke's aunt and uncle might offer you all a place to hide eventually.

'When I went to see Ribke to tell him about your mother, it didn't take too much persuasion. He went off in a flash to Biscobich and the rest . . . Well, who knows it better than you yourself?'

I'd always thought my mother had been too proud to ask Ribke herself in case he said no. But then Rachel's mood changed, unexpectedly taking on an earnest tone, and in a hushed voice she told me the real reason Mum didn't go to see Ribke herself.

'The truth is, she was afraid of her own kind. The Jewish people. To our great shame, some of them turned out to be common informers. They would report to the Germans the whereabouts of hiding places, or tell them if anyone had a plan to escape. They thought by being so treacherous that they and their families would be spared. It made them feel secure for a while so that they could go on, happily rotting away. But in the end, just like everybody else, they too eventually found themselves scorched in Chvalnitz.'

As shocking as all of this was, I felt as if pieces of the puzzle, hinted at by Mum over the years, were finally slotting into place. The story about Ribke, however, didn't end there and I remembered Mum going to talk on his behalf to the kind Bolshevik, gifting him some cognac to sweeten the deal. Rachel and I had a good laugh about this, and she filled in some gaps in my knowledge. I learned that this official had been imprisoned in the first place by the Nazis because he was a socialist. And when the Russians liberated Ludmir, the prison was stormed and all the political detainees were freed. And he was among them and he eventually became a big cog in the new regime.

But it wasn't Mum he knew, it was Dad who, as Rachel revealed, had an interest in socialism, despite running a number of thriving businesses. Today we might label him more of a liberal, but back then he was very different to many of the Jewish men around him, who were more conservative in their views. He believed that men should be free to aspire and to pursue their talents whatever their background. He was open to new ideas and embraced new technology – he was a natural engineer, fascinated by everything mechanical. I knew he had a good head for business but had assumed he was an ordinary Jewish father. He was anything but that.

By now the countryside was shrouded in darkness, and it was time to head for home. This journey passed with more and more questions, mainly from me; but Rachel was so noble that she very kindly answered every one of them. If she found it difficult to think back to such dark times, she didn't show it. My head was spinning with all the new information that had come my way in such a short time, and I felt so happy to be able to fill in the blanks about our past.

The following day, I got up early to set the breakfast table.

I could hear Rachel negotiating the rickety stairs and thought it might be a good idea to leave her in peace this early. So I confined myself to small talk as we sat facing each other. In the occasional silences, I mulled over what I had learned the day before.

I'd discovered that Dad was a true twentieth-century man, which did not suit Grandpa. Out with the tyrannical tsar. He believed in work, bread and freedom for the masses. A new dawn, full of spring promises . . . all taken away in the heat of a midsummer's day by the start of a mad war. I had always known that Dad died so that we could live. When he went up to forage food for us, he met his own assassin, at a time when that killer would have thought that the house was free from Jews. And it was because of Dad's sacrifice that they didn't bother to search for anyone else; they thought he was the last Jew in the building, so we were all spared to live another day. But I hadn't seen until now how his life before the war had saved us.

It was Dad who knew Ribke and gave Mum the idea that Ribke might be able to persuade his aunt and uncle in the country to hide us. The socialist prisoner who had noticed us in the prison yard hadn't called out the names of any of the other people who were queueing to go on the lorry to their deaths. He called out Dad's surname, "Fischmann". He tried to help Dad's family with everything he had – a small loaf of bread. He had the hugest of hearts.

Before we left for the day, I couldn't help but ask Rachel one last question.

'Rachel, you remember all these events that we went through. What part do you think we three children played?'

Rachel fell silent. She pulled out the handkerchief that she cradled in her sleeve and dabbed her eyes. 'Sorry,' she said, 'too much mascara.' As she glanced at me, she said, 'You three were the core of your mum's strength.'

Chapter 21

Bearing Witness

On a spring day in 1982, when I was forty-two, I had just unlocked the front door, laden with shopping, when the phone rang. I dashed to answer it, sensing it was my mother.

'Hi, Mum, you beat me to it. I was just about to call you.'

As I was weighed down with bags, with the floor looking like a branch of Marks & Spencer, I told her I'd call her back in a tick.

'Right,' she said, and put the phone down.

From the unusually brief way she said 'Right', I thought something must be up, so I filled the kitchen worktops with my bags and returned her call immediately.

'Sorry, Mum. I'm in a bit of a muddle here, after all the shopping. I really could have done with you to give me a hand. So now, what's up? I bet you're sitting down with a glass of hot tea and a slice of *lakach* [sponge cake].'

'Just tea,' she said.

As Mum was normally far more expansive, happy to chat about what was going on in her life and the latest political situation in Israel, I began to be a bit concerned. 'What are your plans for the weekend?' I asked. 'Have you been buying carp for your yummy gefilte fish?'

'No, not this weekend.'

'Really? That doesn't sound like you.'

While this strange conversation was going on, I was starting to get worried.

'Sorry,' she said, 'gefilte fish is the last thing on my mind right now. I'm going to Germany.'

'What!' I cried, in disbelief. 'Why Germany, of all places?'

In an odd way, I was relieved that it was only Germany that had altered Mum's mood. That at least meant that things were not as bad as I had initially feared.

'Can you spare the time?' said Mum. 'It's quite a long *spiel* [story].'

'Yes, of course, Mum. I can't wait to hear the *misse* [tale].'

'Good,' she said. 'I'm going to mention two names from the dark past that will certainly mean a great deal to you. Westerheide and Altvater are going to be tried in Dortmund, Germany.'

The district commissar in our region and his sadistic assistant. I felt numb at the very sound of those names.

'You will also be aghast to learn that Altvater had been working in some government office as a welfare officer in charge of youth.'

'*What?*' I exclaimed.

'Yes,' said Mum. 'Giving her the completely unrestricted opportunity to continue spreading Hitler's poison all these years.'

I was stunned. Putting that snake in charge of the young.

The impressionable young. Like clay in the hands of a demon potter. This appalling revelation made me think that Germany might be littered with similar examples, with creatures like Altvater continuing to work freely in government offices. When I thought about it, it was a perfectly feasible idea. Where else did all the Nazis who put Hitler in charge go? They certainly didn't just evaporate into thin air. They were still out there, somewhere. (I subsequently learned that Altvater had married in 1953. Her husband worked for the district youth office in the Detmold, and she had taken over the care of a six-year-old boy, whom she eventually adopted and who as a young man attended her subsequent trials.)

'What an utter tragedy,' I said. 'It's hard to comprehend. But now we know why so many Nazis are emerging once again, on their long march. You know, Mum, the synagogues here have turned into fortresses. They look as if they're under siege. Security guards have to monitor the people who come in. You have to bring identification with you before you come to worship. And, who knows, maybe, in the not-too-distant future, we'll all have to wear a Star of David once again, to point out who we are.'

I could sense Mum's familiar heavy, prolonged, painful sigh coming on. 'Sadly, nothing changed.' I felt her voice understandably becoming melancholic. Time to break this mood and talk brass tacks.

'So Mum, why the rush to Germany?'

'I've been asked to give evidence at the trial.'

I was astonished, after so many years.

'Are you up for that, Mum?'

'Well,' she said, 'to start with, it hit me like a ton of bricks. But once I mulled it over, I said yes. So few of us survived that if I don't go to tell the story, who will?'

After a brief pause, I said: 'Let me know the date of the trial and I'll see you there. Dad would have been so very proud of you.'

Wilhelm Westerheide, then aged 73, and Johanna Altvater, aged 62, had been officially accused of complicity in the murders of 9,000 Jews in the Volodymyr-Volynskyi ghetto between 1941 and 1943. After the war, Westerheide had kept a low profile, living with relatives, passing himself off as a farm labourer. He and Altvater had already been acquitted by a court in Bielefeld in October 1979 after the prosecution had failed to produce enough evidence. During the court proceedings it was said that both Westerheide and Altvater smiled at the cameras and insisted they were innocent. Altvater gave the impression she was a sensitive young woman, just a secretary, who abhorred violence. This was a woman who we knew had thrown children into walls and over balconies, and had lured them with sweets before shooting them – she had always seemed to revel in violence, not abhor it.

When they were acquitted, there was a public protest, and in July 1980 the supreme court decided that the case should be reopened and ordered a new trial to go ahead in Dortmund, a central office for the investigation of Nazi war crimes. The trial started in March 1982 and the chief prosecutor, Hermann

Weissing, had secured twenty additional witnesses to provide testimony.

The other witnesses included Ann Kazimirski, who had emigrated to Canada. She and her husband Henry had survived the 'actions' of the SS in Ludmir by hiding in various attics and a barn, but had also witnessed first-hand the atrocities inflicted on her community, including the shooting of her own mother. Ann and Henry had given evidence at a 1971 trial held in Düsseldorf against SS commander Gunther Hermann and accomplices who were accused of murder, principally of Jewish people in the Ukraine and in Ludmir. The accused included Wilhelm Braune and Waldemar Krause, deputies of Wilhelm Westerheide who had overseen the arrest and executions of Jews in Ludmir. Westerheide and Alvater were not present at the trial as they had not been tracked down. However, according to Ann, Westerheide's name came up again and again as the man who had ordered the accused to carry out the executions and that he was clearly a major player. In 1971 the accused were found guilty and sentenced to prison sentences of between three and a half and nine years.

When Ann Kazimirski stood up to give evidence at the 1971 trial in Düsseldorf, a woman in the audience immediately lunged at her and tried to strangle her, causing the trial to be suspended for a short while until she had recovered. Knowing what had happened to Ann, I was concerned for Mum's safety, but she, with predictable resolve, was adamant that she should go, maintaining: 'That's exactly what they would have wanted – we mustn't let that put us off.' My mother had a need to be at the trial, to say what she wanted to say, and to face the two people who had personally overseen the murder of so many, with the hope that they would finally be brought to justice.

It was a cold day when I left for Heathrow to go to Germany. I was booked on a British Airways flight and was lucky enough to have a seat by the window, looking out as we left land and approached the English Channel, dotted with its huge container vessels. Later on, during the flight, as I was deep in thought, the captain's voice came from the cockpit, informing us of the temperature, wind direction, local time, and wishing us a pleasant flight. I have always delighted in such announcements, being thus reassured that the wings are still intact and no flames are bursting from the engines.

Whenever I flew with British Airways, I tried to imagine the age of the pilots, wondering if some might have taken part in the Battle of Britain, or perhaps finished up as captives in Stalag Luft III.

In Dortmund, I hurried over to the courtroom. As I entered, I immediately spotted Mum, dressed in her charcoal-grey suit with a colourful scarf resting on one of her shoulders. She never plastered herself with lots of makeup; she wore just a thin layer of pale lipstick that emphasized her piercing violet eyes. I was glad to see that my brother Shalom and his wife Elana were already there keeping her company.

While we were all catching up on how we were and inquiring about our separate journeys, the shameless Altvater had the effrontery to actually come across and speak to Mum. She came bearing tedious tales of woe about her dreadful ill-health and how relieved she had been to get away from Volodymyr-Volynskyi. It was so bad that even she could not stand the carnage any more. This from a woman who had helped murder many thousands of innocent people, operating alongside Westerheide and Koch. Her intention, no doubt, was to pacify my mother, so that her evidence would be less damning. Ann Kazmirski, who was also a witness, described Altvater as having 'aged terribly', but I couldn't bring myself even to look at her, nor could Shalom. He felt sick.

Mum graciously kept her composure; in fact, she was the strongest of the four of us.

'Mum, you should have punched her right in the middle of her delicate state of ill-bloody-health. What a shameless bitch.'

'I wouldn't contaminate my hands,' was Mum's reply.

We entered the stark-looking courtroom, which was packed with people, including journalists and students sympathetic to the survivors of the Holocaust. Mum was taken to the main part of the court, while we sat in the gallery above and looked down at her as she waited to speak. Whatever was going through her mind, she appeared extremely composed.

The panel of elderly judges appeared, robed in black, and took up their allocated places. The two accused, dressed in civilian clothes, sat close to this huddle of judges and lawyers, expressing no sign of guilt or remorse whatsoever. If anything, they looked rather sanguine and self-assured, as if already exonerated from any past indiscretions.

When Mum's turn came to give evidence, I felt that the lawyer questioned her in a flippant manner to put her off guard, almost as if she herself were the accused. He opened by asking her: 'What makes you think you possess the right credentials to be a witness? Have you ever met Westerheide and Altvater?'

A resounding 'Yes' came from Mum, who was giving her answers in Polish, which were then translated into German by the interpreter. I don't have a record of exactly what was said, but this is what I remember: 'Unfortunately, Your Honour, I had the misfortune to come across both of the accused. I lived under their cruel regime for three years. They obliterated an entire city. This obliteration included my husband, my two brothers, five sisters, my parents, and the rest of my extended family.'

The lawyer continued: 'Can you tell the court the precise time when all of this allegedly occurred?'

Mum calmly replied, 'That would be rather difficult. We had no means of telling the time as our watches had been stolen from us by the accused. We never knew what time of day it was. In fact, time had no meaning under the rule of the accused. Life as we knew it had stopped; the world had stopped rotating.'

The lawyer then said: 'Can you tell the court what kind of gun they were using to shoot with at the time?'

Mum replied: 'That would be rather difficult to describe as I have never carried a gun and am not *au fait* with such weapons. I imagine the two accused sitting before you would be far better placed to answer that question. And, I might add, in order to kill, you do not always need a gun. Horses' hooves and bare hands can do the same as a gun, like for instance in Westerheide and Altvater's case.'

The lawyer then demanded: 'How many people did the accused shoot?'

Mum answered: 'The numbers are beyond counting. Judging by your age, you must remember what Hitler said – "If we killed just a few Jews, the world will be aghast. If we killed millions, nobody would believe it." It is inhuman. It is inconceivable. So, you Germans went on the prowl and did precisely that. Your people turned Europe into a river of blood, with floating bodies of the dead all asking, "Why?" Perhaps you could tell them, could tell us all, "Why?"'

From this exchange and others like it throughout the proceedings, it gradually became apparent that the evidence presented to the court would not convince the judges of the guilt of the accused. Those who had formerly testified at the trial had faced the same questions again and again from lawyers, designed to throw doubt on their recollections. The earlier trial of 1978–9 similarly failed to reach a verdict, partly because the chief witness, a former junior officer of the Wehrmacht, was unable to remember the colour of Westerheide's uniform at a moment when Jews were being shot in the spring of 1943. It was all too long ago and the details were too vague.

At one point, I saw a younger judge outside the courtroom who seemed to be standing by, perhaps in case any of the older ones keeled over. He spoke some English so I took the opportunity to chat to him as I was interested in what he might think of Germany's less than illustrious past.

'It looks like the two accused are coming out of this without a stain of guilt, although there is so much compelling evidence against them,' I said.

'*Ach du Lieber*, we have to go with the law. They carried out the orders of a legitimately elected government *und* to kill

Jews was legal. Even if the one who gave the orders was raving mad. So, no crime.'

'*Nicht*,' I said, looking at him with pity.

I had warned Mum before the trial not to expect too much, reminding her how many cases came to nothing, with lack of evidence being cited when the judiciary knew perfectly well that written evidence had been torched. If they were not prepared to make allowances for the memories of witnesses being dimmed by the many years that had passed, why hold the trials at all? It felt like a show they were putting on. Mum came out of these court proceedings completely drained. And yet, she felt that she had, at least, shed a lot of the anger that had been buried within her for decades. On 21 December, Westerheide and Altvater were duly acquitted of all charges due to lack of convincing evidence – a verdict that was met by shouting from spectators whom the judges ordered to be cleared from the room. Not once did Mum complain about the sickening outcome of this trial. She did not expect any better in a German court.

I had noted that Westerheide had very clever defence lawyers who must have been expensive – how on earth did he pay them when he had been working as a farm labourer? Out of all the money he looted from us Jews, no doubt.

And what really made my mother's blood boil was that Zavidovich, head of the Jewish police, who had emigrated to America, was not there to testify against Westerheide and Altvater. Thousands of innocents had died on his watch. He was in a position to provide all the facts and figures that no court could possibly have ignored. Perhaps he was afraid of what Westerheide knew about his own actions in the war.

After the trial, Mum had planned to return to Israel, but I managed to persuade her to come back to England with me. She was a great traveller. She loved going places, mostly alone, but occasionally with one of the family. This was the first time in my adult life that I found myself travelling in the company of my mother, so it was a good opportunity at last for just the two of us to have an open, uninterrupted talk, with no hairdresser's appointment!

The trial had of course brought to the surface many long-repressed thoughts about the war years and, during the time Mum stayed with me, we were often on our own and talked about what had happened. There was so much still niggling at the back of my mind. I was still keen to learn more about Ribke and how he had managed to persuade the Yakimchuks to take us in, despite the huge danger it put them in.

'Well, Ribke had a few tricks up his sleeve. The main one was Ivan, a decent guy who'd hooked up with some unsavoury young Ukrainians. He was good with a shovel, but alas, he didn't measure up to his old man otherwise. Although Yakimchuk was a wise old owl, Ivan was easily led. He'd been recruited by the SS to dig fortifications for them.'

'But how did Ribke manage to persuade Mr Yakimchuk to take on our calamitous quartet?' I asked.

'Well put,' said Mum. 'This was where the story really unfolded. Don't forget that this was already November 1943 and the Red Army was fighting to take Kiev. It looked like Hitler was losing and the Ukrainian Nationalists were afraid of what Stalin would do. Ribke told Yakimchuk that the Soviets were almost there, and that the lives of all the mob who had aided the Nazis in any way were in peril. And that, of course, included his son, Ivan.

'When Yakimchuk heard that his only son's life was in jeopardy, he was going to do whatever he could to prevent the disaster, and he agreed he'd harbour a Jewish couple so that he too could look good to the Soviets. But what he hadn't bargained on was being lumbered with a woman and three children. Yakimchuk felt that he'd been tricked; and, as a proud man, it was hard for him to swallow. And for me later on, it made it all that much harder, always trying to make sure that we were not thrown out.'

'Mum, do you really think that Ivan's life was on the line?'

'No, not at all. He was small fry for the Russians. And in the beginning, they weren't going to ruffle too many feathers. They wanted to be seen as liberators, not like the Germans who came as occupiers. But Ribke, he was different. To the Russians, he was the ace in the pack.'

'Mum, I'm so happy you managed to save Ribke.'

'Yes, I know,' said Mum. 'But it could have gone either way. I was just lucky.'

Chapter 22

The Past

Whenever I mention to friends that I love Christmas, they say, 'Surely you mean Hanukkah?' But living in England means I have come to embrace the festivities – in fact, I can never wait for December to come. I love London at Christmas the most, and when the festive lights are on it is at its best. Christmas makes my soul sing. At twilight, when there's a gentle drizzle, the squishy roads cast their spectrum of shimmering lights and it reminds me of the soggy *Parisian Street Scene* by Edouard Léon Cortès. But it was also the time of year when my thoughts drifted back to the past, to Biscobich. I imagine that many people whose lives have been touched by very contradictory extremes – the dehumanization of war followed by the joy of 'normality' – can in an instant, at times of celebration, be reminded of darker times.

During one Christmas visit, I walked with my husband David, hand in hand, through the streets of London, watching men dash into Liberty's for their last-minute presents. On the corner, there was a man selling roast chestnuts. What a treat.

He was warming his frozen hands by the burning coals in his rusty barrel. As I looked at him nostalgically, I thought, I know just how you feel. It transported me back to when I used to warm my hands using a spoon as a home-made lamp, complete with oil and wick, stuck in the earthen wall of a frozen pit.

We stopped to buy some chestnuts. I picked up the brown bag, filled with warm nuts, my husband paid and, after the 'Thank you' and 'Merry Christmas' wishes, I began busily peeling the charred chestnuts, my hands turning blacker by the minute. I chuckled to myself. Just like Mr Yakimchuk when he would appear with the baked potatoes, covered in soot. Mrs Yakimchuk was very cross with him. He didn't like to sweep the chimney. Who would?

Christmas was also one of the rare occasions when my silver cutlery came out. It took a lot of polishing and, once released from the captivity of its accumulated grime, onlookers would require sunglasses to withstand the glare. While polishing, I had a vision of the four of us crawling out from that long stay in the pit. And by then, we would have forgotten that there was light even at the end of the black hole. It would be a bright, sunny July day, and the strange orange sun would be beaming down. And our eyes would be squinting furiously as we asked: 'What was that strange object in the sky?'

David knew about my past, of course, and we both learned more on the occasions when we went to visit Mum. By the early 1990s, Mum was in her eighties. She was still independent and living in a flat outside Tel Aviv, around the corner from Haim, but time was catching up with her and we were aware that she wouldn't be with us for ever. We visited as much as we could, and David always enjoyed pumping her for information. He had a real fascination with the history of the war and, ever the journalist, he was always keen to ask questions about her experiences. The only issue was that David didn't speak Hebrew, Yiddish, Polish or Russian, and she didn't speak English; but somehow they got by, with David relying on his schoolboy German, although I would occasionally have to check certain stories with Mum just to make sure they were correct. At times David definitely got the wrong end of the stick.

I yearned to go back and see some of the places that formed the backdrop to my earliest memories, as painful as they were. But for many years that wasn't possible: the land of my birth had become a part of the Soviet Union, a state that you could visit only under close supervision; you couldn't wander off upcountry and fraternize with the locals. I could have gone on an Intourist package to Kiev, but I would never have been permitted to go in search of my rural roots, and it could have been dangerous for the Yakimchuks if I had turned up on their doorstep.

But then the USSR started to change. In 1990, Soviet leader Mikhail Gorbachev came to Britain and appeared with Prime Minister Margaret Thatcher on the steps of 10 Downing Street. He was sporting a high-end coat fashioned by the most eminent Russian couturier. His wide-brimmed hat was no different from that of nearly every top-ranking Soviet politician of the period, but it was worn at a slightly jaunty angle to the right, perhaps by chance but perhaps to symbolize that the great communist monolith was about to move politically in the same direction.

Mrs Thatcher declared, 'I like Mr Gorbachev. We can do

business together', and thereafter we witnessed a seismic shift in geopolitics. In 1991, the Berlin Wall came down and it was followed by the dismantling of the whole of the Iron Curtain, the barrier that had been preventing my return to Ukraine. I could now go back to Biscobich, finally to see again the god-forsaken dark pit, to touch the frozen subterranean walls within which light never shone and children never sang.

My first assignment was to learn Russian, so that if and when I was fortunate enough to be reunited with surviving members of the family, we could speak to each other directly rather than through an interpreter: so much gets lost in third-party translation.

Once my language proficiency was good enough, I wrote to the church in Biscobich, where Mrs Yakimchuk had taken time off from pounding potatoes into submission. Indeed, I wrote several times, but never received a reply. I next tried to contact some Ukrainians who had fled to England after the war, and I thought I'd struck lucky with a man named Nikolai, who actually came from my old city of Volodymyr-Volynskyi and now lived in London. I arranged to meet him for tea at the Intercontinental in Park Lane.

I was on my third cup of coffee when Nikolai appeared, looking a bit sheepish and bewildered, I thought, by the deep-pile carpet and general opulence of the venue. I was slightly reserved with him, too: why did he leave his native land? I couldn't help wondering. Was he one of the 'Chipko, chipko' mob, the Ukrainian policemen who had hurried us into the ghetto? I chided myself for such unworthy thoughts: he hadn't had to attend this meeting; he was probably all right.

I told him that I was looking for a family named Yakimchuk, and hoped that, being a Ukrainian from Volodymyr-Volynskyi, he might still have some relatives there who could help.

Nikolai's command of English was very Ukrainian, and so was the way he drank his tea. He took no milk and sipped it through a lump of sugar. I was astonished by his apparent unwillingness to embrace his adopted country: even though he had resided in England for many years, and was married to a local woman, he still seemed to live as if London was Volodymyr-Volynskyi-on-Thames.

'More tea, Nikolai?'

He nodded and pushed his cup across to me to fill.

'What made you abandon your homeland?' I asked.

His response was slow and difficult to understand, but I put that down to his lack of English. I took a draught of tea, then asked:

'Nikolai, do you by any chance remember my dad's bicycle shop?'

Instantly he came to life: 'You could not have missed it; it was quite a focal point, right on the main parade.'

He screwed up his deep sunken eyes in an effort to remember the name of the street.

'Farnah Ulitsa,' he finally proclaimed with triumphant glee. 'That was where we would get our bikes and take our girl-friends into the woods to gather mushrooms.'

A nostalgic gaze spread across his well-furrowed face.

'Mind you,' he added, 'our girls were never called Sarah.'

'What is wrong with the name Sarah?' I asked.

'Aah,' he replied, 'Jewish girls with fat legs. They all were Sarahs.'

He came out with a mocking laugh that revealed a toothless gob. I called the waiter for the bill and brought afternoon tea with Nikolai to an abrupt conclusion.

I took a taxi to St Pancras to catch the last off-peak train home. The name 'Sarah' kept ringing in my ears throughout the journey. I wished I'd told Nikolai that my middle name is Sarah and that my legs are not fat and that I am Jewish. But I decided not to because I thought that doing so would just give him an opening for another nasty racist smear.

Unsurprisingly, I never heard from Nikolai again.

I was making poor progress, but I was not discouraged; indeed, my brush with the anti-Semite made me more determined than ever.

Then, in the early hours of the morning on 3 April 1994 came the phone call I had been dreading. It was Shalom, telling me Mum had died. Right up to the end, she had been resilient and sharp-witted, resisting going into a care home until just a few months before her death. She always preferred the company of young people and joked that she was bored by the elderly and their endless tales of medical complaints and troublesome daughters- or sons-in-law.

My brother Haim had travelled to her care home in Haifa the evening before she died. She seemed in fine fettle and, as he left, he remembered Mum waving goodbye from her balcony and then still waving to him as he looked up again from his car, almost as if she had an intuition that it would be the last time they would see each other.

I was determined to get to Mum's funeral, and Haim managed to get it postponed by a day to give me a chance. But a kind man at the travel agency explained that all flights to Israel were fully booked, since Pesach was coming up. I pleaded with him to try, and he did manage to persuade a passenger to make a mitzvah (good deed) and give me their seat.

At the funeral I was astonished to see so many of my old friends there to say goodbye to Mum. There was much talk of her past and her courage. As her body, wrapped in a white shroud, was lowered into her grave, I remember one friend whispering to me: 'You must have your own story; after all, you were there.'

'Yes, I was there,' I said, watching as the last soil was spread, 'but here lies the story.'

Chapter 23

Back to Biscobich

While rummaging through an old diary in 1997, I came across the name of an acquaintance from years past. I suddenly remembered that he had a Ukrainian girlfriend: maybe she could advise me on how I might track down the Yakimchuks. I got in touch with him and explained what I was up to. He was sympathetic and told me he would tell Maria and that she'd get back to me quite soon. I didn't even have to wait that long. Almost immediately, Maria got in touch, wondering how she could help. I asked her if they had telephone directories in Ukraine. She said maybe in the big cities like Kiev or Kharkov, but in the sticks the chances were very slim. But then she said: 'I tell you what. My mother is still in Ukraine. I'll ask her if it's possible to touch base with people who live in the countryside.'

A few days later, Maria told me that her mother could not find the name Yakimchuk in any directory, but she did have the phone number of the central switchboard of western Ukraine and wondered if they might be able to connect me.

I rang the number. A friendly Russian lady answered and I

explained in my limited Russian who I was looking for and the reason for my search. At first I found that her determination and wish to help were infectious, but when I mentioned Biscobich and she told me that the village no longer existed, my heart sank. I could not bear to hear that the heroic barn had capitulated and the pit was gone.

She then explained the reason for Biscobich's demise was that it had been discovered that it stood above a rich seam of coal, and so most of the inhabitants had been relocated to a new town named Novovolynsk in order to make room for a huge colliery.

Still the kind Russian lady said she'd try to find the people I was looking for. 'Give me a couple of days,' she said, 'and I will let you know the outcome.'

Two days later I rang again, and my contact was audibly delighted to tell me that she had managed to locate a Yakimchuk in Novovolynsk. I was over the moon. She gave me the number and, to save me the cost of an overseas call, she transferred me directly free of charge. I could scarcely believe such generosity.

The man who answered the phone at the other end identified himself as Stefan. This was indeed a voice from a very distant past. I explained who I was and asked him the names of his mum and dad. He said Ivan and Manka. Promising, but not conclusive: these are popular names in Ukraine. Then I played my trump card: 'Did your father have a sister?'

'Yes,' he said. 'Paraska.'

That clinched it: this was beyond doubt the child I had met in Biscobich all those years ago. I asked him if any other siblings were about and he said Alexandra, his sister. He gave me her number and shortly thereafter I got through to her on the phone.

I explained who I was, but she was not buying it. She threatened to put the phone down, but I kept going in my rudimentary Russian. I was so close; I wasn't going to be thwarted easily now.

Although she stayed on the line, Alexandra was getting tetchier and tetchier.

'This is the fifth joke call today, and now in some peculiar accent. I've had enough of it.'

I persisted. 'Alexandra, why are you so reluctant to believe that I am the young girl your grandparents kept during the war? No one in their right mind would fake it.'

I started to feel that she was mellowing, and she was beginning to consider the possibility that this was not a hoax after all. Then she pointed out that the date was 1 April, when people play jokes on each other. We have the same tradition in Britain, of course, but I hadn't noticed or thought it would be relevant. After that we laughed for a moment, but then we both wept.

Not long after that my husband and I left for Ukraine, the trip organized for us by an ITV film crew who came along to film the story. We landed in Lviv – once Lemberg – and spent the night in the Grand Hotel, an elegant late-nineteenth-century building. Our bed was comfortable, and David was quickly and annoyingly fast asleep. I lay in the dark, something nagging away at the back of my mind, a feeling of discomfort. In the morning, I was the first to breakfast and said to our waitress, 'What a splendid place this is.'

'It would be, would it not,' she said. 'Only the best for the SS and the Gestapo. You know, this was their head office. A lot of people who come here, just like you, are intrigued about the place.'

I was stunned.

David appeared, clapped his hands as usual and asked enthusiastically, 'What's for breakfast?' I tried to keep a straight face as he pedantically ordered his cup of tea. ('Could I please have my tea in a china cup, not a glass. Yes, with milk, not lemon. Please can the milk be cold? Thank you so much.') To her credit, the waitress didn't roll her eyes. After she'd gone I repeated what she had told me.

'You know, David, my grandma Hannah's family all perished in Lemberg.'

'Yes, I remember your mother telling me. There were so few of your family who survived.' He looked stricken for a moment. 'I was reading that Lemberg had a famously cultured Jewish community of more than a hundred thousand people, and all that remain are a few hundred. It sickens me to say that a Jewish wedding today has more guests than the whole of Lemberg's survivors.'

'Well, we Jews do love a wedding,' I said, feeling brighter. 'It's about time we had another invitation. I would love to give my new Fenwick's hat an outing. It has to earn its keep. I'm sorry, I know I'm being trivial.'

'Don't be silly, I love it when you escape into your day-dreams. It unburdens you for a while. All you survivors carry such guilt. You are always asking, why am I alive when so many others are not?'

My perceptive husband had a rare knack for piercing through a person's defences to see the truth buried beneath. We had time that morning for a quick tour around Lviv. I wanted to see the flat where we'd stayed in 1946, and take in the charms of the city once known as Lemberg. As we looked at the opera house, we thought of the Jewish orchestra at the Janowska concentration camp. These musicians were forced to play the tango during executions, and the foxtrot when prisoners were being tortured. When the Nazis were closing the camp, they made the forty-strong orchestra stand in a circle and play. They shot conductor Jakob Mund first, then forced each man to move into the centre of the circle, put down his instrument and strip, before putting a bullet in his head. We moved on feeling sombre. Then, in the afternoon, it was time to catch our train to Volodymyr-Volynsky. I wondered what would be waiting for me after so many years away. I stared out of the window at the passing countryside, seeing the occasional house in the generally uninspiring vista. I didn't think I would be sending any postcards home saying, 'Wish you were here'. Suddenly there was an ear-splitting screech from the brakes and the train jerked to a halt. My heart was thumping from the shock and even David put his book down. Our fellow passengers in the compartment didn't bat an eyelid. One man shrugged. '*Normalmo.*'

An intimidating conductor appeared and spent what felt like hours inspecting our tickets until I was sure we would be arrested. Finally they were stamped in violet ink and I asked him why the abrupt stop. '*Normalmo*,' he said, and told us an old lady and her goats had been crossing the tracks. Thankfully all had survived.

We were just about to disembark from the train when I noticed a huge sign in bold Cyrillic letters: 'Volodymyr-Volynskyi – A City Celebrating 1000 Years of History'. I had to smile at what seemed like a sad attempt to overlook the past.

The Yakimchuks' offspring met us at the station, where they stood clutching flowers for us. I did not remember much about the city of my birth; it looked very shabby and unloved and I was glad not to be part of it any more. We went to see where our old house once stood, on a road that I always knew by its former Polish name of Horodelska. There was no other house in its place, just an empty mound, although it was surrounded by other houses and bungalows. I tried to engage with the locals but they shied away: was it because of their participation in the atrocities, or was it because they feared we'd come to reclaim the land that had been stolen from us? Perhaps it was because of communist propaganda: before the advent of glasnost, Soviet people regarded Westerners as enemies. At first I felt sorry not to be able to chat with people, but on reflection I decided that I didn't mind. I felt well out of it; they were welcome to their blood-sodden earth.

We were then taken to Stefan's home. It was packed with the Yakimchuks' children. There were not enough chairs to seat us all, but Stefan soon solved the problem. He ran out to the yard and reappeared with a long plank of wood on his shoulder. He then positioned a chair at each end of the long table and placed the well-seasoned plank on top of them to accommodate all the diners, who then feasted on pickled herring and potatoes boiled in their skins. The table did not buckle under the weight of the bottles of vodka that were piled on top of it, but the sound of it groaning might not have been a product of my imagination. I asked Stefan why there were so many drunks on the street and he told me it was because vodka was cheap and they were encouraged to drink to forget their unhappy lives.

After our sumptuous feast, we piled into Ladas and went to what had been Biscobich. There we could not fail to notice a huge wheel churning out black coal. Stefan had an old plan that showed where the Yakimchuks' old house and barn had once stood. But there was no sign of it now, nor – of course – of our previous residence, the pit, nor yet of the calamitous attic where we heard a boy telling his uncle that he knew he was hiding Jews.

Our lives had been in the hands of this one small youth, Symon, and to my elation, the Yakimchuks took us to see him in a nearby village. Up until then I hadn't known if he was still alive. He was much older, as were we all, and I was thrilled to be reunited with him. When we got to his place I was over-whelmed by the warmth of his embrace. I was sorry that it had taken so long to meet and thank him for being so gallant at such a tender age. He took us to greet his wife, who looked perplexed by all the excitement. The couple welcomed us with grace and generosity. Their abode consisted of one room that housed two single iron beds. In the corner was a clay oven belting out black smoke.

We were entertained royally. Symon's wife laid on a fine array of bread, tinned sardines and more bottle of vodka. I was a little sorry that I was teetotal and not able to sample the dif-ferent flavours on offer. Symon sat on one of the beds and I on the other. I was captivated by his stories of what went on in old Biscobich while we were in the pit: some of his tales were hilar-iously funny; it was clear that Symon was a great storyteller and knew how to spin a yarn. Some of his other tales, however, were hellishly brutal. He told us that during the first and second pogroms, people from the village and surrounding area would rush to Piatydni if they heard shots or knew something was going on so that they – men, women, children and even Symon's own family – could watch the killing. It is impossible to understand why anyone would want to witness such horror. Harder still to understand why, the whole time that Symon knew his uncle was harbouring Jews, he kept silent.

Symon also recounted the story of Yakimchuk's reaction when his nephew told him that he knew there were Jews in his barn. The old man grabbed him by the ear and told him not to mention it to a soul, especially not his mother.

Symon felt his ear as if to make sure that it was still there. 'Yes, it is,' he said with comical relief, 'but I still feel the pain to this very day.'

I couldn't help thinking, Yes, Symon, so do I; pain was our daily diet at that time. But I kept that to myself, saying instead:

'You know, Symon, my mother did tell me this story, but it sounds to me so fresh in the way you tell it in Russian. Mum spoke a lot about you. She admired your young bravery: children of war grow to be courageous just like you. She would have been delighted to have seen you now, but she left us not so long ago. It is such a shame she did not live to meet you; this would have been such a great get-together. Mum had a long life, a hard life; she was dealt some rotten cards but she was unbreakable and fearless.'

Symon cracked open a fresh bottle of vodka and shed a tear for Mum.

'Yes,' he said, 'she was all that and more.'

Perhaps the time that meant the most to me on my journey

of discovery was the hours I spent alone with Alexandra (or Sasha), without the extended family at her parents' – Ivan and Manka's – old home. As I approached the tiny, solitary cottage, I saw her waiting for me, a willowy middle-aged woman with striking Nordic features and blue eyes, just like her mother Manka. Her wavy hair was held back by a white metal comb decorated with bright enamelled flowers.

Sasha showed me the cottage's well-tended garden, with neat rows of cabbages and potatoes, as well as apple, plum and cherry trees. She told me that she made the journey from her flat every day to tend to the garden, her refuge from the demands of everyday life. She invited me to see inside the house, where Ivan and Manka had seen out their days after they were forced off the farm to make way for the colliery. As soon as the front door opened, I had an image of Ivan with his shovel, digging us out after our pit collapsed, and of Manka in her Easter attire, bringing us water in that chipped black pot.

Sasha and I sat on one of the two shallow beds that stood in the single-room house. Suddenly she jumped up saying, 'Before I forget, I must pick up something.' She went out and I found myself thinking again about the Yakimchuks and why they had helped us. Was it to protect Ribke and Ivan, as Mum believed? Was it Mrs Yakimchuk's saintly soul? Yes, both are true. Mr Yakimchuk was not as saintly as his wife (but then, who is?), and yet I believe he was a good person who cared what happened to us, whatever his original motivation was. As I sat there I asked myself, as I so often did, why did we survive when millions did not? The only answer I can find is that perhaps we were spared so we could tell the world of the sick madness that engulfed Europe, to join our voices with the other survivors and remind future generations what happens when we allow fantasies of racial superiority and hatred to take root.

Sasha came back carrying two large jars of jam made from the fruit of those trees Ivan and Manka had planted and nurtured when they first came to live here.

'These are for you to take home,' she said.

I thanked her, moved by her kindness and by the idea that I would be taking a sweet taste of Biscobich back to England with me. As she wrapped the jars carefully, I told her it reminded me of the time her mother smuggled us knitting needles hidden in very similar yellow cloth.

'Oh, I know this story off by heart,' she said. 'My mother always told it at Easter. She could have paid with her life if she was captured, and even the dog would have been shot as a collaborator!'

The two of us were laughing. 'It was not funny fifty years ago,' Sasha said, wiping away a tear.

I was so glad I'd learned enough Russian to speak to Sasha without an intermediary, to laugh and cry with her as we remembered the past.

It was Sasha who told me that Mr Yakimchuk, that brave old soldier who loved Haim and at times was ready to escape the war with him, had gone on to live to a very great age and died just a month or two before his hundredth birthday. His wife had long predeceased him.

According to Sasha, as he was dying, a tear left his eye and he said, 'I wonder where those three children are now?'

What had struck me most forcibly when I was in Symon's

house was the small, solitary window looking out on the killing fields of Piatydni. That image stayed with me when I went on to the memorial to the Jews of Volodymyr-Volynskyi who were murdered in the Holocaust: a large obelisk on top of which sits a hunched woman with her head bowed in sorrow. I thought of my mother grieving over the loss of my father, and of so many members of our family, and I took out my prayer book, intending to say Yizkor, the prayer of remembrance. But then I began to ask myself what kind of entity I was actually praying to: what all-powerful yet supposedly benign being would permit such inhumanity? How could I praise him? I wondered. I closed the book in anger.

It had been getting dark as I stood there. A star came out, then another, and then the moon, until the sky was filled with infinite and majestic light. And I thought, who am I to question all of that? I was just a speck of cosmic dust. Millions before me had wanted the very same answer, so why should that eternal mystery be revealed now to me?

I slowly opened up the book again and said the words I had heard so many times:

'Lord, what is man, that thou regardest him? Or the son of man, that thou takest account of him? Man is like to vanity; his days are as a shadow that passeth away. In the morning he flourisheth, and sprouteth afresh; in the evening he is cut down and withereth. So teach us to number our days that we may get us a heart of wisdom . . .'

Epilogue

Past and Present

The effect of past trauma never leaves you. It is deeply buried in one's subconscious just waiting for the right opportunity to break free. 2020 was the year that unleashed a deadly virus on mankind, Covid-19. As the pandemic swept the world, it took away my freedom and unlocked a door to the past I'd tried to keep closed. Even so, without it, I would not have written this book.

My husband David died in 2014 after fifty-one years of marriage, leaving me feeling hollow, although I tried to conceal this. When life seems empty, company is so very precious and I was looking forward to my son Avi's visit on 22 March 2020. The old refectory table was set for lunch, and I even remembered to fill a jug of water with ice cubes, a slice of lemon, a twist of lime and a sprig of mint from the garden. It's not like me to be so far ahead – I seldom plan, probably as a result of a childhood marred by unpredictability. With a few moments to spare, I switched on the television to catch the latest news bulletin. There was panic buying in supermarkets where shelves

237

were stripped bare. Schools had closed. It was predicted that hospitals would soon be overwhelmed.

Caught up in troubling thoughts, I was relieved to hear the sound of the doorbell. I quickly switched the telly off, trying my hardest to conceal my angst as I opened the door. There was my son, with a smile on his freckled face as always.

'Come into the warmth, Avi. Its looking like winter refuses to give way to spring.'

'What's for lunch?' he soon asked.

It didn't take long for Avi to demolish the plate of food – he is such a fast eater! At times, I have to apologize for holding him back. After successfully spilling my coffee on a freshly pressed table cloth, it was time to face the kitchen sink. We had a short debate over who was washing and who was drying, and then I was ready to pump Avi for the latest family news. He bought me up to date about Max and Louis, my grandsons, who would soon be graduating from university, and their girl-friends. I do love hearing what's going on in their young lives but, however joyous, these visits never seem to last long enough. After telling me about Max's latest cricket exploits (he scored a 100!) and Louis's trip to Paris, Avi had to dash to the gym. 'I must lose weight,' he said, while emptying a box of chocolates. Just before he left, he told me, 'Mum, don't be glued to the television because it will make you sick.'

I waved Avi goodbye from the window. When his car was no longer in sight, I made myself a cup of coffee and thought how lucky I was to have a son not too far away, especially since my daughter, Elaine, couldn't have gone further afield if she tried. She lives in Australia but we are fortunate to see her every year and remain in constant touch, which makes such absence easier – as she says, 'I'm only a phone call away.' However, these were not normal times and she was prohibited from flying. We stuck rigorously to the rules, unlike the rule makers . . . It would be almost three years before I saw Elaine again, which was hard.

After a long, wakeful night, I was glad to open the blinds, put the kettle on and brew a fresh cup of coffee to watch with the BBC News when, suddenly, a red alert flashed across the screen: *Breaking News – we are now in lockdown.* My heart sank. Lockdown? Not again. The loss of freedom, the feeling of being caught up in frightening events beyond one's control reawakened dark memories. When, at one of the Downing Street daily press conferences, medical director for England Stephen Powis said, 'If we keep the death toll below 20,000 people, we will have done very well', I switched the television off. I felt utterly numb. This is when I decided to follow Avi's advice not to be glued to the news for the sake of my sanity.

Avi still came to see me, although we followed the advice on social distancing until the government allowed single people to be in a bubble with another household. As the months passed, the fear lessened, especially when news came that the Oxford AstraZeneca vaccine had been developed. Adversity always manages to bring out the best in human ingenuity.

Life had become repetitive with visitors so restricted, which is the reason I reacted the way I did when, towards the end of the year, I stumbled across a documentary about Princess Alice. As I flicked through channels, avoiding the news, my eye was caught by the dashing Prince William at Yad Veshem, the Holocaust memorial in King David's royal city of Jerusalem. The prince was talking passionately about his great-grandmother, Princess Alice of Battenburg. I didn't know very much about her, but the documentary revealed that she was born in Windsor Castle and later married Prince Andrew of Greece and Denmark. She was living in Greece when it was invaded by the Nazis and she bravely harboured a Jewish family in her home. When searches were carried out by the Gestapo to find Gentiles hiding Jews, she was the last candidate to be suspected. Her son-in-law, Prince Christoph of Hess, was a member of the National Socialist German Workers' Party (NSDAP) and the Waffen-SS so, in the eyes of Hitler, she was a true Nazi banner waver. But Alice herself was cut from different cloth – she was as far removed from Nazism as Hitler and co were from sanity. She was completely and wholeheartedly devoted to the Greek Orthodox Church. She cleansed herself of all material possessions, giving them away to charitable causes, mainly through the church. She had lost a daughter, the biggest tragedy that can be inflicted on a mother.

I was deeply touched by Alice and almost felt I had encountered her in my distant past. Then I realized that her story reminded me of Mrs Yakimchuk. Her country, Ukraine, had also been invaded by Nazis, she was a devout member of the Orthodox church like Alice, and she too secretly harboured a Jewish family. And all this while her house was commandeered by the Gestapo and SS to train young Ukrainians, including her son. She must have seemed like a true collaborator to the Nazis and was not even remotely suspected of providing a safehouse for Jews. She also donated all her material possessions to the church and suffered the tragic loss of her only daughter. And yet, she always praised God, saying, '*Slava, Slava*' (Glory, Glory).

Epilogue

Alice and Mrs Yakimchuk came from such different backgrounds, and yet they had so much in common. One was royal by birth, the other truly noble by nature. Princess Alice's story is well-documented, being Prince Philip's mother and the mother-in-law of Queen Elizabeth II. Mrs Yakimchuk's story, by contrast, is hardly known. That is when I had what seemed at the time like a mad idea: why didn't I write a book about Mrs Yakimchuk, she deserved to have her courage celebrated. The idea fired me with enthusiasm and I started writing the very next day, although I soon realized at the heart of our family story was another women, Rivka Fischmann, who happened to be my mum. A woman with extraordinary grit who was fearless in facing adversity.

It took me the best part of two years to finish the book, and I hope I have done justice to Mum and Dad, Mr and Mrs Yakimchuk, Ivan and Manka, Ribke, Stacha, the two valiant Wehrmacht officers and all those whose deeds are celebrated here. The Holocaust is the biggest act of genocide humanity has seen. It was conceived in the heart of Europe, the continent that gave birth to the Enlightenment and to some of the greatest minds in science, art, music and literature. Alas, it also gave birth to a corporal of little schooling, who possessed of a sick mind, and a remarkable gift of spreading venomous hatred. Genocide can happen anywhere – it has happened many times in the past and it is happening right now in Ukraine, on the very soil that saw such suffering eighty years ago. We must remember the past. We must learn to stand up for what is right rather than follow the masses. We don't have to repeat the same mistakes again.

Acknowledgements

I want to thank my friend, David Lipman MBE, who was the first to read the initial draft. He was full of encouragement and fired up my enthusiasm to bring it to print. I shall be indebted to him for life for his unwavering support.

My greatest thanks go to my literary agent, Annabel Merullo of PFD. I was stunned when she rang to offer me a space in her stable. I'm so humbled that she had confidence in the manuscript and we soon found four publishers bidding for the book.

I'd like to thank Emlyn Price, my first editor. We worked for nearly two years on the manuscript, which was handwritten and posted via Royal Mail between us. We had a great working relationship – we coined it the 'Mutual Admiration Society'. Until this very day, I have still not met Emlyn in person as we worked through Covid and weren't permitted to share the same space. I do hope to meet him very soon to reminisce about the good times when the two of us were part of the 'Mutual Admiration Society'.

Acknowledgements

This is also my opportunity to thank David Wilkinson, the producer of *Getting Away with Murder(s)*, for introducing me to Emlyn. He was a brilliant find!

I also thank Henry Russell, my second editor, who finished editing the manuscript when Emlyn was busy on another assignment. I'm full of admiration for Henry who had the 'chutzpah' to send the manuscript to Annabel. Thanks, Henry!

All my thanks go to my neighbour and friend, Stephen Miles: a chartered engineer, an ace racing driver and the photographer who took my photo for the jacket of the book. As I am computer illiterate, he became my port of call for all emails. He was also part of the long and tiresome journey that was the initial transfer of the book from paper to the computer and has been involved with *A Mother's Courage* for the last two years. He even makes sure my old battered car, better known as 'Dimples', which has been the victim of altercations with bollards in the wrong place (never my fault), is not starved of fuel. In fact, he was going to top up the tank with the special refined petrol used in racing cars but when I told him I had just received a speeding fine, he suggested I take the bus. I still owe him an apology for ruining his state-of-the-art computer while watering my garden enthusiastically while he was working silently on the other side of the fence. I managed to spray him and his computer with a torrent of gushing water!

My sincere gratitude goes to Ingrid Connell, publishing director of Pan Macmillan, who drew the short straw and had to endure my computer illiteracy. She is the epitome of politeness. In her bank of words, 'no' never appears – she always says yes. However, it took me a while to realize, that her 'yes' is

Acknowledgements

occasionally a big no! Her charm and enthusiasm are infectious. I am so privileged to know her and have her as my editor. My biggest regret is serving Ingrid a lumpy risotto, destined for plastering a crack in my wall.

I would like to thank Emma Marriot for her input and research. It was invaluable and much appreciated.

Appreciation also goes to all those who sail in the Macmillan ship, including editor Lydia Ramah, Charlotte Tennant, who made the text perfect, Lindsay Nash, for creating an elegant text design, and Neil Lang for the beautiful jacket. And also to the publicist, Chloe Davis. It has been a pleasure to work with you all.

And finally, all my thanks and gratitude go to Avi – he is my strength and stay. I am so blessed to have him as my son. I am deeply grateful for all his support, care and, most of all, his sense of humour that at times creases me up. Thanks, Av, for all of the above.

Last, but not least, thanks go to my daughter Elaine, for planting a mad idea during one of our long-distance phone calls from Australia during Covid: 'Why don't you write a book during Covid to keep you sane?' I listened to her advice with sincerity but, alas, sanity is still an open verdict!

About the Author

Malka Levine was born in Ukraine but moved to Israel in 1948. She is widowed with two children and lives in Nottingham. She appeared in the Central TV documentary on her return to Ukraine, *Malka's Story*, and the C4 documentary *Getting Away With Murder(s)*, an investigation into why so many perpetrators of the Holocaust went unpunished. *A Mother's Courage* is her first book.